Serpent at the Door:
The Films of P.T. Anderson

by

Steven Martinez

ISBN: 978-1-304-04917-9

Table of Contents

Introduction:

FLAWED GODS
and LOST MEN

*

Among the anecdotes surrounding the manic process by which P.T. Anderson's third film came into being is a tale concerning William H. Macy's cabin and a snake. Anderson had secluded himself in his friend's cabin, high in the towering mountains, to complete the screenplay for 'Magnolia.' Like any other writer Anderson experienced moments when he longed to escape the burden of creative labor. Given the massive scope of the film, expectations were high. The project could not move forward without a finished screenplay, and Anderson was making precious little progress. For him the pressure was greater still given the critical acclaim of his previous effort, the whirlwind 'Boogie Nights.' But escape was not an option for Anderson because (as he muses in the 'Magnolia Diary') an ominous snake had appointed itself sole guardian of the only doorway out. This compelling figure would not grant him the freedom of escape; so Anderson sat, and persisted, and wrote — keenly aware of the watchful serpent outside.

Now, the veracity of this anecdote is not especially important, but the fact that Anderson chose this story to communicate his creative struggle is illuminating because it reveals the manner (and symbolism) by which he naturally imagines drama. Understand, his frame of reference here is biblical. The imagery it conjures depends on our immediate association between serpents and original sin, temptation, and knowledge. These touchstones power much of his artistic thinking and creative sense of expression, as they certainly did throughout the filming of 'Magnolia.' His comprehension of biblical imagery informs not just the process by which that film came to fruition but forms the basis for interpreting all six of his major films thus far.

Whether discussing the introduction of Sydney to John in his first feature film 'Hard Eight,' or the serendipitous meeting between Jack Horner and Eddie Adams in 'Boogie Nights,' or the deliberate obstacle that Eli Sunday represents to Daniel Plainview in 'There Will Be Blood,' P.T. Anderson, in almost every film, has carefully crafted a tableau of human movement born from (or reacting to) the broad theme of divine intervention. It is the towering specter overlooking all his films, and the network through which he communicates himself as an artist. Further, this arc of divine intervention, so subtle in its evolution over the course of his six films, is the prism through which Anderson grants his characters a profound inner light, or self-awareness.

In the body of his cinema, Anderson consistently breeds a unique dynamic between flawed gods and lost men. These relationships (and those peripheral to them) operate at the extremes. Sometimes one character is granted total authority over another (as in 'The Master'). Sometimes one is allowed to gradually usurp the other's power (as in 'There Will Be Blood'). In many instances Anderson's figures move away from a blind acceptance of fate toward a greater reliance on free will. Each of his films is distinct, but they all share dramatic features that depend upon divine intervention and the relationship between flawed gods and lost men. How these figures find (or fail to find) redemption, love, or personal solace forms the substance of his filmmaking.

It might be argued that this interpretation, so reliant on themes of divine intervention, relegates Anderson to the status of religious artist (a nom de plume that nowadays might be counted against him). However Anderson's concept of 'gods' is not so literal as might be surmised by common phrases like 'biblical,' and 'divine.' Rather, he filters a representation of divinity through flawed men and coincidental circumstance. From the Bible he only borrows moral implication and storytelling technique to suffuse his drama with gravity. The meeting of flawed gods and lost men in almost every instance propels Anderson's characters into journeys of discovery. They encounter good fortune, fall from grace, and are eventually (to varying degrees) redeemed. It is Anderson's deep fascination with imperfect figures—and their inability to function within accepted social networks—that motivates his art and binds him to common human frailty.

*

This is not an interpretation of Anderson's films based on anecdote or biography, nor is it an interpretation based on the director's thoughts regarding his own work. Rather it's an interpretation based on a careful study of the films them-selves; a monumental body of work fraught with angels and demons, bound to earth by Anderson's affection for the Everyman. His first six films may someday be understood as a dedicated unit; each of them crafted around the actions of flawed gods and lost men, impelled by divine intervention.

Some will argue that this interpretation seeks to superimpose the Bible over a model of artistry that is actually secular; and that divine intervention should be more correctly understood as chance, or fate. But the consistent reference to divine signs and symbols, so ubiquitous in Anderson's films (save perhaps one) reveal a deep—even subconscious—reverence for the Good Book. This is sometimes manifested overtly, as in the figure of Eli Sunday. In other instances it's more subtle, as in the selection of 'Niagara Falls' as the retreat to which John and Clementine flee from their earthly paradise in Reno.

My argument is actually straightforward: that P.T. Anderson is an artist whose primary mode of expression emanates from a biblical understanding of human motive and action. The depth and strength of that expression girds the architecture of his films, from 'Hard Eight' to 'Magnolia' to 'The Master.' His entire canon is given its primal spark in the very first scene of his first major film, where Sydney (the flawed god) introduces himself to John (the lost man) without invitation. This distinct instance of divine intervention marks the beginning of a long, regenerative, journey.

It should be noted that Anderson himself has never discussed his collected films in the context of divine intervention, nor has he expounded the notion of flawed gods and lost men. My argument is not meant to be taken as a definitive interpretation (as though such a thing were possible) based on the director's pronouncements. Rather my perspective derives from a personal attempt to better understand his art, fully aware that the path to interpretation is traversed by the individual alone. We each approach art with our own warehouse of experience and intuition; and we each forge interpretations as a bridge to the piece itself. This book is the result of my own approach to Anderson's unique body of work, born out of respect and admiration. It proceeds from the premise that the artist himself has no dominion over the manner by which his work may be interpreted once it leaves his hands. Images and words, plot and composition — all become vulnerable to interpretation by virtue of the fact that art is only an arrangement of abstract medium, the imprint of which can never be perfectly consistent in the minds of those who observe it.

Anderson's medium is image, word, and sound. That he chooses certain words over others implies a deliberate effort to imbue his narratives with structure and direction. In 'Magnolia,' his crafting of the phrase: "The Book says we might be through with the past, but the past ain't through with us," is unquestionably purposeful. His choice to alter the 'Watkins' family name in Upton Sinclair's 'Oil!' to 'Sunday' in 'There Will Be Blood' is also purposeful. Further, the visual symbols he chooses — whether the graceful pools of water in 'Boogie Nights,' the impossible rain of frogs in 'Magnolia,' or the grueling baptism in 'There Will Be Blood' — reveal an effort on the part of the director to make certain connections in the viewer's mind. Those connections generally derive from a biblical point of origin; channeling its resonant themes to deepen the imprint of his cinema. By doing so, Anderson (quite intuitively) has developed a timeless, universal sensibility that consistently unearths human drama from the womb of Western culture.

This brief introduction lays the foundation for an interpretation of Paul Thomas Anderson's films. It's a platform from which a cohesive exploration of his cinema can be launched. In surveying his six major films (and two early shorts) Anderson's implementation of divine intervention should be understood as intrinsic to his artistry. Further, it should be understood that the artistic ends to which he employs this powerful device become more complex as Anderson himself matures. This increased sophistication emerges through a gradual effort to imbue his films with a greater sense of tragedy born from the difficult relationship between fate, will, and personal consequence.

A meeting between flawed god and lost man propels the action of his first major film. That journey proves ultimately rewarding for all concerned. By the end of his most recent work however, that same dynamic leaves his protagonist in total ruin. In every film between, Anderson's carefully wrought narratives reveal a divine hand guiding each purposeful encounter. Even before his first major film, a specter of divine intervention was already surrounding his cinema. It is precisely this phenomenon that Anderson described in his 'Magnolia' anecdote: an imposing, fearsome, serpent at the door.

Here we go.

Prologue:

FIRST FILMS

*

By the time P.T. Anderson finished high school he had completed his first film. This precocity is not unique among filmmakers, but what distinguishes Anderson is the sure instinct he displayed for the medium even at this early age. His first short films would in fact become the basis (though greatly enlarged) for his first full-length features, 'Hard Eight' and 'Boogie Nights.' Thus his work was already of such quality that it could withstand being lengthened and broadened, yet retain its drama. His natural talent for writing emotionally rich (if flawed) characters is also evident. By placing them in difficult circumstances (generally of their own making) Anderson further reveals a grasp of human folly. In these two small films he displays a maturity well beyond his years.

Perhaps "experimental" is the most useful phrase in describing these short works, especially for those principally interested in his major films. Both 'The Dirk Diggler Story' (1988) and 'Cigarettes and Coffee' (1993) reveal an artist still learning his own aesthetic preferences—not just technically, but in terms of ideological pronouncement as well. Every filmmaker makes choices concerning what he wants to convey through the medium; whether tragedy, comedy, hope, loss, faith, perseverance, or whatever. Assessing these short films in context, one aspect that reverberates strongly is just how philosophically different they are from his major films. As might be expected, Anderson used these short works as a laboratory to experiment with certain themes and modes of expression in an attempt to learn what his own artistic 'voice' would be. This is doubly true since Anderson has always written his own scripts, making him solely responsible not just for how these films look but for what they say. More than anywhere else, it is in the finale of each short film that the sharpest distinctions can be drawn between this early phase and the later (mature) period of Anderson's filmmaking. Above all, these closing moments reveal a much more pessimistic artist than would later emerge.

*

When he was only 18, Anderson completed 'The Dirk Diggler Story,' a 31-minute film tracing the rise and fall of a young porn-star whose name the title bears. The film is constructed as a mock-documentary, which seems a harbinger of Amber Waves' self-conscious documentary of Dirk in the later, greater, 'Boogie Nights.' Again, so certain are Anderson's instincts that nearly all the principal characters who would later appear in that film are already fleshed-out here. Dirk Diggler, Reed Rothchild, Jack Horner; all are present in this little movie, almost without alteration. Even the actor playing Jack, Robert Ridgely, turns up again in 'Boogie Nights' as the ill-fated Colonel.

Appropriate to the length of the film, the story is fairly simple. Dirk is discovered by Jack at a falafel stand, asked to do some modeling work, and before long is introduced to the world of pornographic filmmaking. Like Mark Wahlberg's Dirk Diggler, this early incarnation (nicely played by Michael Stein) grows drunk on his own star-power. He develops a volatility that finds release through fits of rage, drug-use, and self-destructive behavior. Ironically, things begin to go wrong for Dirk just when he becomes most successful. Given an increase in notoriety and earning power, his ambition grows beyond his talent. He's become too big for Jack Horner; and the two part company on bad terms after a botched film-shoot. Dirk attempts to finish the film himself, but can't complete it.

He then records an unremarkable rock album, which only fuels his ego. To a great degree he's in a self-contained universe here; convinced of his own celebrity whether the rest of the world acknowledges it or not. Quickly his appetite for drugs becomes insatiable, much to the lament of his good friend Reed Rothchild. Deeply unsatisfied, Dirk dives into the world of legitimate action films, starring in a TV pilot called 'Angels Live in My Town.' Unfortunately (if predictably) the pilot bombs, and Dirk is left humiliated not just by this failure but by a string of unsuccessful ventures. Unable to fund his overwhelming drug-addiction, he returns to the seedy world of pornography. Sadly, because he's burned so many bridges and proven so unstable, gay porn is the only work he can find.

At this point Jack Horner exhibits great sympathy for Dirk's plight. In a poignant moment he recalls the successes Dirk brought him during their early years together, reflecting: "I saw someone who had given me everything he had to give, when I realized that I hadn't given him anything." This selfless gesture represents a distinction from the Jack Horner of 'Boogie Nights.' Here the character actively rekindles his relationship with Dirk because he feels he owes him a second chance. In 'Boogie Nights,' Jack initiates no such gesture.

They do indeed reunite, and a new porn film is quickly scheduled. All signs point to a glorious return to stardom for Dirk. Jack even leads the crew in a quiet prayer, asking the Lord to bless their efforts. It is thus the height of irony that, just before filming commences, Dirk is found dead in his dressing room. Jack's prayer goes unfulfilled, and instead the film ends with a montage of sad remembrances set to Barbra Streisand's 'The Way We Were.' One of the crew-members sums up Dirk's legacy rather bluntly: "It wasn't until now that I realized what a terrible inferiority complex he had."

'The Dirk Diggler Story' is a short film made by a young artist, and should not be subjected to the same level of scrutiny required for a full-length film. But understanding some of the distinctions between this early effort and 'Boogie Nights' is crucial because they provide insight into Anderson's rapidly developing aesthetic.

First among these distinctions, and one of the most important, is the ultimate fate of the protagonist. Here, Dirk is found dead in his dressing room due to a drug overdose. He's not permitted a return to grace nor is he allowed to resume his successful lifestyle. Anderson instead pulls the rug out from under him just when he's come home to the place he belongs. This rather cold ending is quite different from the much more generous circumstance afforded the later Dirk of 'Boogie Nights.' In that film, Dirk is allowed to return to Jack's good graces. He's given the opportunity to continue doing what he loves most with those who truly care for him. Despite the heartfelt remembrances and memorial music, there's a naked cynicism to 'The Dirk Diggler Story' that does not manifest itself in 'Boogie Nights.' Granted, Anderson may have simply wanted to fashion a mock-cautionary tale; one in which self-destructive behavior begets self-destruction. However this approach, on an ideological level, is very different from Anderson's later allowance for forgiveness and redemption.

The second key distinction concerns the element of romantic love. Here, there is no romantic sub-plot to match the deep and rewarding love that develops between Buck and Jessie in 'Boogie Nights.' That romance is born out of good fortune and emotional honesty. In 'the Dirk Diggler Story,' by contrast, no true love develops at all. The only character who harbors any inkling of romantic feeling is Reed Rothchild. Yet his love for Dirk is only hinted at, and never requited. This absence of romantic love is very rare in P.T. Anderson's work, and again suggests a much colder, harsher, artistic intent than would inform his later films.

Most important of all, assessed in the context of Anderson's canon, is the lack of spiritual presence. In almost all of his films Anderson routinely employs a sophisticated palette of divine intervention and biblical symbolism (what I refer to as 'flawed gods and lost men'). This is particularly true for 'Boogie Nights' which makes constant reference, both through image and dialog, to religious touchstones that imbue the narrative with spiritual purpose. Yet here it is virtually absent. The only moment when any spiritual guidance is invoked comes during Jack Horner's prayer near the end, and that lone instance (though spoken sincerely) is played for a laugh because it's so absurd. Contrast this with the utterance by Burt Reynolds' Jack Horner during the hot-tub scene in 'Boogie Nights' (discussed later). Here, in this early work, the absence of any divine undertone is very stark indeed, and contributes to the film's vacant atmosphere. This critical distinction reveals Anderson's incomplete artistry at this point in time.

It can be argued that the reason some of these themes are absent is due to the film's short length. Meaning, there simply wasn't enough time to develop a romantic subplot, let alone construct a template of divine symbolism. It can also be argued that Dirk's death was Anderson's effort to give the film a certain finality; an unambiguous end. But again, the product of the artist's vision—however short or long—exemplifies his aesthetic pronouncement. If Anderson harbored a sensibility that granted romantic love a priority, then he would have included it in his film; even if only for a single scene. The same is true for divine symbolism.

More critical is the absence of any redemption for Dirk himself. His ultimate fate, and the cruel manner by which it strikes, speaks to Anderson's easy cynicism at this stage of his artistic development. If he believed in the promise of human redemption, then he would've granted it to Dirk instead of insisting on an empty death. This is not to say that Anderson, as a person, didn't believe in redemption; but rather that he didn't place a priority on expressing it through his art. This marks a profound contrast with his later preference for bestowing upon his characters an enormous charity. As will be shown, he consistently grants them forgiveness, redemption, even resurrection, in the wake of hardship and failure. To sum up, it might be said that Anderson possessed great talent at this point in his young career — but did not yet possess great wisdom.

*

Only a few years later, Anderson completed a more serious film entitled 'Cigarettes and Coffee' (1993). It too is quite short, clocking in at 24 minutes, but here the quality of writing and maturity of design surpass anything found in his previous effort. The structure itself reveals a startling degree of sophistication given his mere 22 years of age, revolving a trio of stories around a vaguely linked set of circumstances. None of the three stories overlap one another in the body of the film. They all exist independently despite the fact that each is joined by a most peculiar symbol: a wandering twenty-dollar bill that bears the name of one of the characters. The sharp, clipped dialog expresses a more immediate sense of personal interaction — more direct and uncluttered — than that crafted for 'The Dirk Diggler Story.' The film communicates a strong feeling of electricity that reveals not just a director of high enthusiasm, but one of great potential.

The narrative itself is minimal. The film opens on two men at a coffee-shop engaged in anxious dialog. A younger man named Douglas speaks to an older (unnamed) man who stoically listens to an unfolding story. The older man speaks of ritual: he wants to hear the story only after his cigarette is lit, and coffee is poured. He's a man of few words, yet exudes a sense of world-weariness. Douglas begins his story. It is fragmentary and incoherent; he can't seem to summon the words to convey the awful implications. Before he can reveal himself completely, Anderson moves on to another couple at a nearby table; this time a pair of newlyweds. Their story too is fragmented and somewhat breathless. It becomes apparent that the young wife has a gambling problem, and her husband is upset. The emotions here are strained, and a sense of their brand-new marriage being tested dominates. Again Anderson cuts to another story. Outside the coffee-shop, a shady figure is speaking cryptically at a pay-phone. His conversation is one-sided. The audience is only permitted to know what he says, not what he hears. Most evident is the aura of threat, or danger.

It is within these three stories, cutting back and forth, that Anderson constructs an interlocking sequence of personal confession—caught at midpoint—that reveals the hidden flaws each character possesses. Just as Douglas slowly confesses his sin to the unnamed older man, so too does the film slowly unveil its secrets to the viewer. More is learned about each character and how they come to terms (or fail to come to terms) with decisions they've made. The film possesses both mystery and symbolism, yet like 'The Dirk Diggler Story,' it stands in contrast to Anderson's later, more mature work. Indeed, when assessed in the context of his entire output, 'Cigarettes and Coffee' concludes the experimental process begun in that previous film; and is most notable for being artistically distinct.

The story returns to the main characters: Douglas and the unnamed man. It's clear the man has heard Douglas's story at least once, but he wants to hear it again. He's not in a hurry; he wishes to allow the matter to unfold in its own time. He seems unwilling to move the narrative along at a faster pace than necessary. Douglas, by contrast, is nervous. He wants to confess himself, both to purge his sin and to receive advice from the older, wiser, man. It's very tempting to refer to this older man as 'Sydney,' because a character nearly identical to him turns up again in Anderson's first full-length film, 'Hard Eight.' In fact, 'Cigarettes and Coffee' is certainly the inspiration for that later film in much the same way that 'The Dirk Diggler Story' is the basis for 'Boogie Nights.' In this short film however, the older man, so perfectly rendered by Philip Baker Hall (who plays Sydney in 'Hard Eight') is never named, nor is he named in the film's credits. Therefore he will continue to be referred to as the 'unnamed man' here.

A striking feature of the dialog between Douglas and this unnamed man is its lopsided sense of urgency. The older man simply will not be rushed into any conclusion concerning the younger man's story. Instead he brings a Zen-like attitude to the conversation, a kind of 'let things be as they are' philosophy which assigns Douglas's story a position in the cosmos — simply one of many lights. Douglas becomes frustrated by his seeming indifference, imploring: "Co-incidence, speculation, right and wrong; you must have more of a feeling than just speculation." To which the unnamed man merely replies: "I'm not sure at this point." In the next breath, he goes even further toward a philosophical mantra, telling Douglas: "I'm glad you're not coming to me for advice as to what you should believe. That's your decision." In this way he declares an unwillingness to play a part in Douglas's fate.

This is perhaps the first appearance of a theme that predominates Anderson's major films. The concepts of fate, chance, and coincidence all play an enormous role in his larger cinema. But in those later films, fate and coincidence are nearly always conveyed through the prism of divine intervention; and they almost always proceed to a place of forgiveness or redemption for the principal characters. Here, Douglas is not so lucky. He (like Dirk before him) is afforded no second chance, or saving grace. Again, this pessimism makes 'Cigarettes and Coffee' a distinctly experimental work when compared to Anderson's proper canon.

Douglas's story possesses an ominous quality. While in Las Vegas, with his wife and another couple, he wrote his name on the back of a twenty-dollar bill. This was just a habit of his. He gave the bill to a friend, Steve, whom he and his wife were meeting that night. Douglas returned to his own room a little later, where his wife had been resting, and discovered that very same twenty-dollar bill lying between the bed and the nightstand. The implication was clear: Douglas's wife cheated on him with his best friend, Steve. Douglas was devastated. He took the twenty-dollar bill, gambled it, then used the winnings to hire a hit-man (named Bill) to murder both his wife and Steve.

Now, in relating this story to the unnamed man, Douglas expresses remorse. He regrets his decision, which will no doubt end in the death of his wife and friend. Before the conversation goes any further, however, Anderson cuts back to the man at the pay-phone outside — who turns out to be this very same hit-man, Bill. He enters the coffee-shop where Douglas and the unnamed man are conversing, purely by chance, and asks the cashier for cigarettes and coffee. He pays for the items with the same twenty-dollar bill bearing Douglas's name on the back, which he obtained from him as part of the payment for the murders. This occurs even as Douglas (just a few feet away) tells the unnamed man: "I can't let my wife and friend be killed. I know I can't get back yesterday, or even this morning. . . I'm really scared. I don't want this to happen." At his point, a remarkable coincidence occurs. The waitress serving the two men brings the unnamed man his change. Among the bills is the very same twenty-dollar bill that Douglas just described. Instantly, the unnamed man realizes that the hit-man (Bill) must be somewhere nearby, meaning that he can alert Douglas, and perhaps they can prevent Bill's imminent murders. But the unnamed man, so opposed to any form of intervention, commits one of the most selfish acts in any of Anderson's films: he crumples the bill — not allowing Douglas to see it — and drops it to the floor. By doing so, he becomes the opposite of an agent of change. He does not permit Douglas the possibility of altering his own fate, or reversing his earlier mistake. Indeed, the unnamed man becomes Fate's assistant, declaring through his actions that a person's decisions must proceed to their consequences. In short, the unnamed man will not intervene in Douglas's destiny.

*

In the closing sequence, Anderson draws the threads together. All five characters—the two couples plus Bill—are linked by this odd twenty-dollar bill. The hit-man pays for his cigarettes and coffee with it, then it is returned to the unnamed man in the form of change, then he crumples it and drops it on the floor so that Douglas won't see it. Only then does the young wife (of the newlywed couple) spot the bill as they leave the coffee-shop. She stoops to pick it up, and they proceed to the exit. In the parking lot outside, Bill the hit-man opens the trunk of his car, revealing the bound and gagged figure of Steve. He quietly intones: "Almost home, Stevie."

The last meaningful words in the film belong to the unnamed man. This Zen-like figure, who affords Douglas no guidance or intervention, merely states: "Just drink your coffee, smoke your cigarette; because that alone will make everything right." These words are the equivalent of 'Just do what you're doing, and whatever will be will be.' By removing himself from Douglas's decision-making process, this unnamed man makes himself not just an agent of fate, but an active agent who ensures the consequences of Douglas's actions are meted out. Because those consequences involve the murder of two people, the unnamed man represents a very dark figure; both detached and uncompromising. It is around this dark figure, and his ironic actions, that the film's themes of coincidence and fate revolve. He allows events to play out as predetermined, for better or worse.

This foreboding conclusion is very different from the manner by which Anderson resolves his later narratives. There, he almost always employs the theme of free will to bring his characters a sense of redemption. But like 'The Dirk Diggler Story' before it, 'Cigarettes and Coffee' ends in death—not onscreen, but through the implied actions of Bill the hit-man. In many ways it's a fatalistic film; one very unkind to its characters. It displays a helpless pessimism that does not match the more hopeful vision of Anderson's mature work.

Again, these distinctions make it clear that 'Cigarettes and Coffee' (like its predecessor) marks a period of experimentation for Anderson; one that displays an aesthetically cynical outlook. In both films fateful decisions lead to fatal consequences, and death is the penalty for bad choices. Harsher still, no force is permitted to usurp that final judgment. Indeed, in 'Cigarettes and Coffee' Anderson goes one step further: he makes his main character, the unnamed man, an active agent of fate who physically ensures nothing disrupt Douglas's regrettable destiny.

This character, who ironically forms the basis for Sydney in Anderson's first major film 'Hard Eight,' is in fact Sydney's opposite. That later character opposes fate both through the purposeful guidance he provides John, and through the erasure of a past sin. More about that in the next chapter, but suffice it to say that Anderson must have rethought this character from the inside-out, along with his own artistic intent, to create so thematically different a film as 'Hard Eight.'

The last aspect of 'Cigarettes and Coffee' that should be discussed is the biblical symbolism which forms the conceptual center of the film. This is especially important when assessing it in relation to Anderson's major works. Like those later films, 'Cigarettes and Coffee' relies upon a biblical theme to provide gravity for its orbiting characters. Without this gravity the film runs the risk of spinning out to nowhere, becoming a disjointed set of stories that bear no relation to one another. But Anderson shows maturity here. The twenty-dollar bill which touches each character becomes not just a unifying symbol, but a platform for thematic moralization. The phrase 'money is the root of all evil' almost certainly informs the substance of this symbol. It is the film's central message, shrewdly implanted in human currency. So completely identified with money are the main characters that Douglas's signature appears on the bill. The hit-man's very name is Bill. The newlywed's marriage itself hangs on the wife's dysfunctional relationship to money. Money is the overwhelming force in these people's lives, and because it brings tragedy to each of them, it must be considered evil.

Think of the scene in which Douglas tells the unnamed man that he used the winnings from that twenty-dollar bill ($8,000) to hire the hit-man. Evil spawns evil in this sequence; multiplying money into more money. That money then literally leads to death. Similarly, the allure of money lies at the center of the newlyweds' problems. When the young wife picks up the twenty-dollar bill at the end of the film, the implication is that she'll gamble it away—perhaps losing everything, including her marriage, in the process. It is this same twenty-dollar bill that earlier revealed the secret of Douglas's wife's infidelity. It informs Douglas. It motivates him. It provides him a guidance well beyond that which the unnamed man offers. In this way the twenty-dollar bill becomes the sixth character of the film; without question the symbolic 'villain.' This prominent placement of a biblical symbol in the body of the film becomes a template for Anderson's later art. Biblical symbolism, divine intervention, and spiritual resolution run strongly through his canon. Those themes are all rooted in this small film. That he designed so sophisticated a device, at such an early age, marks the arrival of a considerable talent.

Indeed, Anderson's next effort—his first major film—reveals an artist fully matured. The ideology and expression contained in 'Hard Eight' surpass anything in this short film many times over. It might be surmised that by working through the process of making 'The Dirk Diggler Story' and 'Cigarettes and Coffee,' Anderson learned what he didn't want to say as an artist. Those films resonate with pessimism; they seem ruthless in their portrait of unyielding fate, and both end in death. By contrast, his later films resonate with life, redemption, and love. It's tempting to imagine that the reason Anderson made these films so short is that he didn't believe their philosophy merited longer treatment; they did not deserve the privilege of being full-length films. The pessimism they embody is exactly where he did not want to steer his art. They reveal a filmmaker still experimenting, still seeking his voice. It's safe to say that both certainty of idea and uniqueness of voice manifest themselves completely in his next film.

Part One:

HARD EIGHT

*

By the time Anderson began writing the script for his first major film, he had certainly decided to fashion the narrative around a character derived from an earlier short. The unnamed man who forms the center of gravity in 'Cigarettes and Coffee,' seems reborn as the principle character in 'Hard Eight' (1996). Again Philip Baker Hall portrays a world-weary man of amassed experienced; but here he is given the name Sydney. In fact, Anderson himself refers to the film as 'Sydney' rather than its accepted title 'Hard Eight' (which takes its name from a difficult roll of the dice). This peculiar disparity between Anderson's preferred title and its actual title suggests the competing ways the film can be interpreted. Some would argue that 'Hard Eight' is indeed a more appropriate name given the prevalent themes of gambling, chance, and fate. But greater scrutiny reveals a more powerful motivating force in determining the film's sequence of action; one that truly justifies Anderson's preference for understanding the film as 'Sydney.'

In the opening shot—in fact the opening shot to all of Anderson's major films—the principal characters are brought together through divine intervention. The choreography immediately establishes the position each character will occupy within this relationship. John Finnegan, humbly portrayed by John C. Riley, is seated outside a coffee shop—a lost man of no material means. Sydney, the agent of change, approaches the man from above while Anderson holds the shot from the diminutive John's point-of-view. He gazes up at Sydney as one would discern a divine, descending figure. Philip Baker Hall lends the character of Sydney an autumnal quality; cloaked in wrinkles born of hard living. In this opening scene it is he who commands the exchange, steering the lost lamb John back into the coffee-shop; prepared to make him an offer he must not refuse.

By framing the shot in this special way, Anderson tips his hand. He's established a relationship not unlike that of a biblical parable. A stranger reaches down from above to shepherd a lost and disaffected soul into a better world. The conversation which follows, within the sanctuary of the coffee-shop, sets their journey in motion.

John mentions losing some money in Las Vegas, and when Sydney presses him it's discovered he needs six thousand dollars for his mother's funeral. Sydney offers to help. When John expresses reluctance, he quietly compels the younger man to come with him to a land of opportunity; a paradise where John might find some greater fulfillment, even redemption. Sydney implies that anything is preferable to drifting the streets aimlessly. But John accuses Sydney of pretending to be a kind of saint: "What are you, man? You think you're St. Francis or something?" From his lips to God's ears, Anderson has indeed conceived this guardian figure in the guise of a saint.

The funeral, mentioned as the reason John needs six thousand dollars, provides a framework around which Anderson builds a sympathetic character. In that opening scene, over the course of just a few seconds, he imbues John with a soul. He gives him the humility to yearn for a proper, respectful, resting place for his mother. Because Sydney sincerely wants to help this forlorn figure, he too gains immediate acceptance into the viewer's good graces. Anderson casts these character in the mold of journeymen, each seeking a different kind of spiritual comfort.

It will not become evident until the last act of the film, but this divine figure, Sydney, is flawed. His providence at this point seems entirely benevolent, but Anderson's characters are seldom 'clean.' They often bear heavy baggage, even if their deepest secrets are not revealed immediately. The inevitable revelation of Sydney's secret—and how it affects the principal characters—signals the arrival of Anderson's full maturation as an artist. The conception of this hidden demon, and how that demon informs Sydney's every action (together with the consequence of its revelation) confirms Anderson's capacity for creating substantive, three-dimensional characters.

A word about the film's imagery is warranted, particularly since this is Anderson's first major film. In these opening scenes Anderson displays a sure grasp of space and composition—whether framing the desolate skies of the American West, the chaos of the Vegas casinos, or the physical movement of his characters. At this early point in his development, his rollercoaster camera-eye has not yet begun to soar and swoop. Rather, Anderson displays the discipline of a learned craftsman determined not to let his characters, or their story, be overwhelmed by camera technique. No, in this first film Anderson is a jeweler shaping his figures with great care; avoiding the glare of artificial polish or magnification.

The static expression used to great effect in 'Cigarettes and Coffee' seems the template for his visual style here as well. Because 'Hard Eight' is in many ways an outgrowth of that earlier short, Anderson's themes strike a familiar tone: money, chance, fate, and the consequences of bad decisions. Unlike 'Cigarettes and Coffee,' these themes are given a purposeful role in securing each character a rewarding resolution.

As promised, Sydney leads John to Las Vegas; land of a thousand lights. His intent is to guide the younger man to a higher plane of personal wealth. Once there, Sydney begins his good work, shepherding his protégé through a warren of sights and sounds; the earthly paradise where John hopes to discover some prize. He soon acquires a confidence of movement, of swagger, not unlike a child who learns to walk for the first time. By the grace of Sydney's guidance, John soon amasses a small pool of wealth. Sydney can sleep easy because the first phase of his work is done. His flock, his creation, has been guided to safety — worlds away from the cold limbo of the coffee-shop in the opening scene. Not to be forgotten, Sydney calmly intones that the six thousand dollars John needs for his mother's burial can be arranged. In a foreshadowing moment he declares: "I want you to see that my reasons for doing this are not selfish, only this. . . I'd hope that you would do the same for me." Overwhelmed with gratitude, John replies: "I would." He eagerly straps down the velcro on his sneakers, and follows Sydney out to the gambling tables. Although he doesn't know it yet, he will indeed help Sydney attain a sense of redemption by the end of the film.

This opening segment of the film, an overture of sorts, brings partial closure to their individual journeys. Anderson uses this early moment of closure as a punctuation mark. He quickly moves the narrative forward by two years, where the pair have formed a relationship that is best interpreted as a bond between flawed god and lost man. At this point in the film, Sydney is a still a divine kind of mystery. We are not permitted to know anything about him, or his past. Nor are we permitted to know any of his motives. We are only allowed to consider him a harbinger of new life to a lost soul. John is not just his cherished lamb, he is in fact Sydney's creation, given the means to succeed through the coming of his figurative 'creator.' This makes John a symbol of the biblical Adam. Sydney delivers this new man into the Paradise of Nevada, where anything is possible and everything is within reach. Except a woman. Sydney comprehends this lack of conjugal harmony; and from this void emerges the biblical figure of Eve, represented in the narrative by Clementine (warmly portrayed by Gwynith Paltrow). The setting is now Reno, Nevada.

*

Like John, Anderson presents Clementine as a lost and wayward soul; a lamb among the wolfish throng who prize her solely for her feminine assets. She's not a particularly talented individual, nor does she display the kind of awareness that might shield her from the base motives of callous men. She's an innocent; a proverbial blank slate. She knows Sydney well, however, and he knows her – she even refers to him by an appropriate nickname: 'Captain.' Indeed that moniker implies authority over aimless vessels in uncharted waters. At this early stage in their relationship, Clementine has no idea how pervasive that authority will be.

In addition to Clementine, Anderson introduces Jimmy, a high-voltage gamesman vividly portrayed by Samuel L. Jackson. A character of high contrast to Sydney, Jimmy is a boisterous misanthrope who fits easily into the casino world of bright lights and shady deals. It comes as no surprise that Sydney doesn't care for Jimmy; a detail that foreshadows an ominous turn of events later in the film. Indeed, suspicions run high when Jimmy mentions having seen Sydney lay a bet on the 'hard eight' many years ago. He's a disruptive presence; too little is known about him, and he forms a wedge between Sydney and John. But really, from Anderson's perspective, he represents the biblical symbol of knowledge in the film; a slick serpent whose dark revelation brings the angel Sydney crashing down to earth – just as the biblical serpent brought down Adam and Eve when they supped from the tree of knowledge.

In the meantime, Sydney takes it upon himself to rescue the wayward Clementine. Like John before her, Sydney seeks some redemption in the task of shepherding her to a better world. But Sydney displays weariness in his efforts, even caution. Where once he dominated the big-money games, now he's content to play minor diversions like keno, causing Jimmy to remark: "What's that, a sign of aging?" For Sydney the clock is ticking; he has little time left in the world. His actions are those of a spent man seeking absolution—and it's through John (and now Clementine) that he means to attain it.

Thus far, John has done well. This is not the same forsaken figure moored outside the coffee-shop in the opening scene, rather this is a man who's found a place in the world. Sydney's done his utmost to provide for this creation of his; a strenuous effort to say the least. In turning to Clementine however, Sydney discerns a much greater emotional difficulty. She requires a certain sensitivity to draw her into his sphere of influence. It's fair to say Sydney's motives become ambiguous here, since Clementine has little to do with his desire to attain a personal sense of forgiveness (although this isn't revealed until later in the film). Rather, his intentions toward Clementine derive from a more straight-forward attempt to unite her with John in the paradise he's created.

Anderson successfully manages each of these characters' unique psychologies, bringing them together in a manner that feels emotionally authentic. He displays a working knowledge of bruised or wounded personalities; anticipating his later films which reveal even greater depths of psychological difficulty. While those films routinely involve large-scale narratives with many moving parts (sometimes incorporating high symbolism and abstract expression), here Anderson's preference is for smaller scale realism. If anything, 'Hard Eight' is most closely modeled on Film Noir, with its gallery of characters who reveal (or are forced to reveal) more and more about themselves as the film progresses—much to the surprise of the viewer.

Anderson's most fundamental aesthetic principal centers on the personal journey of flawed characters. The struggles of these characters — both physical and emotional — form the basis of all his films. Rarely does he exhibit a desire to infuse his cinema with wild abstraction, or surreal impression, or even chronological tinkering. Instead, he remains focused on character. In terms of setting, Anderson prefers to delve into the more obscure facets of society. His stories do not take place within functional offices, or universities, or upscale restaurants. In terms of visual style, he always fashions images around the momentum of his characters. For him the stylistic flourish of a film should never be promoted above the people in it, rather it should serve their collective interaction. This tenet is not just evident in 'Hard Eight,' but every film before or since.

It should come as no surprise that Anderson often champions the anti-hero (as here, with Sydney) given that he came of age during a decade of anti-hero filmmaking. 'Hard Eight' is not a product of the Hollywood system, nor does Anderson come from the inner-sanctum of established studios. Rather, he developed an independent approach to filmmaking, and revered those directors who learned their art by crafting personal work. 'Hard Eight' is indeed a personal work, spawned by an encyclopedic knowledge of, and passion for, cinema. In particular, that cinema which shines a light on the disaffected and dysfunctional — but also the found and forgiven. The small pleasures and inner-pains these characters experience form the backbone of Anderson's cinematic body. In his first major film he lays down a marker for the humanity he wants to portray, and has remained devoted to that purposeful humanity ever since.

'Hard Eight' contains the inner-conflict and human drama that signal enduring art. Sydney's personal journey is arduous, and filled with sacrifice. Things go wrong along the way, almost to the point of ruin. But at the heart of his motives lie basic human truths. His desire to attain redemption for past sins, and a selfless urge to perform some good deed before it's too late — these are powerful devices in human storytelling. The worlds Anderson creates, in 'Hard Eight' and elsewhere, are fraught with lonely souls who overcome great difficulty to find a place they can call home. Throughout the span of Anderson's canon he imbues ordinary settings with extraordinary magic; and it's worth noting that from the very beginning he greatly prefers, artistically prefers, the triumphs and tragedies of flawed gods and lost men.

*

As Sydney sets out to save Clementine, the scene shifts again to a dim coffee-shop, deliberately recalling the opening shots of the film. Clementine jokes with him about John's unshakable attachment: "He orders the same drinks as you, you know. He dresses the same." This is a symbolic reminder that Sydney has successfully shaped John in his own image. The conversation becomes more serious when Clementine confides her desire to live day-to-day without having to prostitute her body. This is truly a decent request, and once again Anderson here (as he did with John) imbues his creation with a soul. Clementine, in this short span of a minute or so, earns our genuine sympathy.

Later, in a darkened motel room, Sydney makes his motives clear. The slow pulse of a tolling bell (used again during a tragic sequence in 'Boogie Nights') signals an anxious atmosphere, and the imagery suggests sexual indecency. But in truth Sydney doesn't want to sleep with Clementine, he wants to rescue her. His desire for redemption trumps any sexual motive, here substituting spiritual solace for physical pleasure. Above all he's a symbolically divine figure whose needs are not materially construed. His work is larger, more intent on bequeathing a legacy and redeeming past sins. To that effort he's done well. Thus far he's created an 'Adam,' but his Paradise can only be complete with an 'Eve.'

Of course, Anderson never makes things easy for his characters. Nor is he content to portray action or decision free of consequence. There's a component to his artistry that demands his characters suffer—just as the Serpent seduced Eve to eat from the Tree of Knowledge, ensuring a lifetime of struggle. This biblical understanding of human trial colors Anderson's art with the hue of religious parable—whether it be Sydney's battle against personal demons here, or the redemption afforded Daniel Plainview, or the hell endured by Freddie Quell. It is this same spiritual lens through which Anderson constantly wrestles his own artistic demons; determined to engage them no matter how difficult the struggle. At the end of 'Hard Eight' a unique metaphor forms the closing image: one drop of blood on the white cuff of Sydney's shirt. In this image lies the sum of Anderson's concept of struggle. It does not simply represent the blood on Sydney's hands, but the spilled blood that emerges from physical and emotional conflict—all of which make up a significant part of his artistic palette. Echoes of the Old Testament inform Anderson's notion of trial and endurance, pain and suffering. They are preludes to the hope of human redemption.

*

And so his creations suffer. The most pivotal scene in the film, about midway through, comes in the form of a terrible turn of events. Sydney is called to a motel room; John and Clementine are inside. What happens next is going to turn his world, and theirs, upside-down. Anderson holds the camera on Sydney as John explains the tragic matter. Slowly, Sydney's face shows a gathering anguish that gives way to an evacuation of hope. John and Clementine have taken a hostage—a man who bought Clementine's services, slept with her, and refused to pay. Now the hostage is unconscious and bloody. Worse, Sydney finally sees his two creations for what they really are: imperfect, careless, and deeply flawed. John bursts into tears: "I'm sorry, Syd. I fucked up—I know, I know, I'm so sorry!"

Now Sydney must do the unthinkable and pronounce a judgment on them. Like Adam and Eve in the Garden of Eden, these two suddenly comprehend shame and humiliation as they face their creator. He's disappointed on the deepest level. How were they lured into this evil circumstance? The sudden stress affects Sydney so deeply that for the first time in the narrative he curses. Here crude language reveals a facet of his character previously hidden — the first of many revelations to come. Still, it's Clementine who bears the greatest shame, just as Eve was made to humble herself in the Garden of Eden. And indeed, Sydney levels his wrath against her: "I did not get you here, so you humble yourself!" This scene conveys the cruelest sense of loss, completely robbing Sydney of the faith he placed in these two fallen figures. "Where did this thing go wrong?" he asks Clementine; but in truth he's asking that of himself. Complicating matters even further, John blurts out that he and Clementine are now married.

But what can Sydney do? He must take pity on his creations. He can't turn his back on these impetuous children, particularly after John expresses that he and Clementine are deeply in love. He confesses to Sydney: "We've been seeing her for two months, and I never had the guts to say anything; then I saw her on my bed this morning and it was like a sign from Heaven." In reality, their union is a carefully orchestrated outcome managed by one of Heaven's symbolic agents. Sydney can't allow their newborn love to disintegrate; he's invested too much of himself in their wedding.

An exodus is hastily arranged; a banishment of sorts from the earthly paradise of Reno. It's a breathless string of events which upsets everything Sydney hoped to gain from this special relationship. Now it's turned to dust, and he must contend with his failure to secure a personal redemption. Adding insult to injury, it's also revealed that Jimmy knew of

the films of p.t. anderson

these foul events, suddenly making Sydney the odd-man-out; the only one not aware of John and Clementine's vile behavior. Again, this cloaks Jimmy's activity in a mysterious veil; seemingly everywhere at once. It also confirms him as the representative figure of knowledge in the film; here possessing greater awareness than even Sydney.

In the last scene before they leave Reno, it's no accident that Anderson selects Niagara Falls as their chosen destination because it allows the word 'fall' to enter the film's thematic vocabulary. The biblical Fall of Man, emanating from the act of eating from the tree of knowledge, here forms the narrative framework for John and Clementine's fall from grace, and inevitable exodus. In a moment alone with Sydney, Clementine confesses: "Oh my God, I'm so embarrassed. Oh my God. . ." Despite their matrimony, the lives of these two will never be free of sin. The next scene is all the more heartbreaking. Sydney, alone in a motel room, watches their wedding on videotape. It's an ironic memento of the happiness that now seems forever lost.

But the great irony in 'Hard Eight' comes in the revelation of Sydney's original sin. In a dark parking lot he's mysteriously called to meet Jimmy, a dangerous figure by this point in the film. It's an uneasy scene, for Sydney sees Jimmy as nothing more than a raw opportunist. In truth, Jimmy's revelation has very little to do with himself and everything to do with Sydney. He accuses Sydney of covering up a bloody past; a past rooted in the streets of Atlantic City. More to the point, he declares his knowledge of Sydney's murder of John's father all those years ago. Sydney is not the guardian angel he's pretended to be—so far above earthly motive—rather he's a fallen angel; a man with a murky past whose present-day actions derive from a selfish quest for absolution.

In this stunning scene Jimmy becomes the surreptitious judge. He turns to Sydney with devastating sobriety: "You think you can just walk through this life without being punished?" Like a thunderbolt, this un-expected revelation of Sydney's past sounds a common theme throughout Anderson's films. The timeless truth that the past can never be completely forgotten; that it always stays with us as a reminder of original sin. This theme is articulated later (appropriately enough by Philip Baker Hall) in Anderson's 'Magnolia:' "The Book says we might be through with the past, but the past ain't through with us." Sydney's unspeakable past — like the past of every man who seeks personal redemption — has finally caught up with him. It's brought him down to earth. This purposeful repeal of Sydney's divinity is crucial to understanding Anderson's art, because it exposes his suspicion of overt angels and a yearning to unmask flawed gods.

This episode also strikes a profound chord in the viewer because now the ugly truth is known. Sydney's murderous past levels the playing field, eliminating any notion of 'good guys' and 'bad guys.' Now there are just human beings dealing with mistakes, and sins, and efforts to make things right. Again this reveals Anderson's preference for finding drama in the day-to-day struggles of fractured individuals. Sydney is a man plagued by remorse, haunted by misdeed. He has no choice now but to throw himself on the mercy of his accuser. He begs Jimmy: "Please don't tell John." Jimmy listens, even complies, but it's going to cost Sydney dearly. Cold hard cash; the currency of the underworld.

Ironically, the amount he finally gives Jimmy is six thousand dollars – the exact amount John needed to bury his mother at the beginning of the film.

In the aftermath of this humiliating extortion, a brief phone call informs Sydney that John and Clementine are making their way home. This creates a renewed sense of urgency in Sydney, for his wandering children are returning to their Paradise. He must prepare for their arrival, particularly in light of Jimmy's revelation concerning John's father. Over the course of this phone call, John reassures Sydney that he loves Clementine very deeply, and that she loves him. In that moment, Sydney decides to lay his cards on the table, confessing: "I love you, John. I love you like you were my own son." It's a satisfying scene filled with requited love; one which bears witness to the halo of kindness Anderson eventually bestows upon his cherished characters. A useful metaphor, when assessing Anderson's cinematic depiction of human optimism (especially when it pertains to love) is Pandora's Box. Just when his narratives seem overwhelmed with chaos, with defeat, a small glimmer of hope shines beneath.

Sydney's last push for redemption comes in an act of deliberate regression. It's a wonderfully ironic scene in which his desire to obliterate his own past comes not in a renunciation of his former self, but in an assumption of his previous identity. His willful reenactment of the man he once was, to become the man he wants to be, is Anderson's thoughtfully orchestrated escape route for Sydney. It reveals an alert writer; here depicting a fallen character who must resurrect his former self to preserve his current standing with John and Clementine. Their love symbolizes Sydney's one worthwhile act on this earth; his one good deed. Their marriage is his redemption — and if his own past (embodied in Jimmy) threatens that redemption, then that past must be destroyed.

Thus, as Sydney waits for Jimmy with a loaded gun, Anderson reincarnates his former self. Sydney emerges from the shadows and annihilates Jimmy without remorse; filling him with furious lead and reclaiming the extorted loot. That amount, six thousand dollars, was earlier needed to bury John's mother — in essence, to bury his past. Here it's reclaimed to bury Sydney's past. He has his money back, but more importantly he's erased his sordid history and secured his present identity.

Which in turns provides an avenue to grace. By defeating his demons, Sydney's ensured the permanence of his one good deed — the union of John and Clementine. And in a film teeming with unexpected revelations, it's fitting that Anderson fashions the final shot around an image of mindful irony. Sydney returns to the very same coffee shop where he first approached John. This symbolic return closes his circular journey and represents a 'homecoming' for the film. The setting symbolizes both a beginning and an end, forming a framing device that calls to mind biblical parable or ancient drama. Sydney sits alone in the shop, calm and reflective, when he notices a lone splash of blood staining the cuff of his white shirt. He quietly covers the stain with his coat, symbolically hiding his bloody past — just as he hid it from John and Clementine (and just as Anderson hid it from us). It's a striking image that speaks to the Film Noir roots of the narrative; upsetting the viewer's preconceived notions of motive and character. In his desire to end the film on that precarious image Anderson declares, purely through visual means, that no man can run from his past. It's always there to remind us of our failings. He sums up our unbreakable link to the past—and the consequences that descend from it—in that one image of Sydney's sleeve.

At the same time, even though Sydney could not run from his bloody past, he was able to keep that blood from spilling onto the lives of loved ones. His love of John and Clementine not only secures his redemption, it provides his salvation. Sydney will never be free of sin or guilt, but in the arc of Anderson's narrative he may be granted salvation through the gift of requited love. This redeeming quality of love is common to Anderson's sense of resolution throughout his canon. It also marks a profound reversal of the pessimism found in his earlier movies. Again, Anderson's short-films were little more than experiments. His graduation into major motion pictures inspired a rethinking of his art; resolving itself into a deliberate shift from simple cynicism to a deeper, more rewarding belief in human redemption. At this early point in his career such subtle optimism marks the emergence of a generous filmmaker; one whose sympathy for everyday people would illuminate his cinema.

Part Two:

BOOGIE NIGHTS

*

Though skillful and entirely possessive of its own visual flair, there is little in P.T. Anderson's first film that would prepare audiences for the kaleidoscope of his second. 'Boogie Nights' is a great leap forward in sheer visual scale, revealing an artist whose ambition behind the camera fully complemented his talent as a screenwriter. After an incubation period of a year and a half, Anderson unleashed a fusillade of visual sweep and taut dialog, ascribing a wild variety of emotions to nearly a dozen major players. This is an instance of Anderson the composer opening his orchestral palette from the chamber-scale of 'Hard Eight' to the full scope of a symphony; exploiting every note he'd learned from his prior effort to tell the story of a notorious industry which, in the end, is not so different from any other.

Anderson's uninhibited approach works to the film's benefit precisely because pornography itself is uninhibited. It's the full-frontal openness of pornography that gives Anderson the green light to shed any sense of cinematic restraint. At the same time, the narrow demographic of so small a segment of society keeps his narrative tightly focused, preventing it from spinning out of control. The social milieu of pornography in the 70's is essentially an island; a secluded kingdom where few pursue relationships outside their own clique of sexual partners. Everybody seems to know everybody else in this exclusive empire, which in turn cultivates an isolated psychology. For all its whirling thunder, Anderson is basically telling the story of an enclave; a 'small-town' replete with cloistered, emotionally naïve, characters who just happen to be sexually demonstrative.

His choice of material is reminiscent of Martin Scorsese's mobsters in 'Goodfellas;' again an isolated community where a specialized set of rules apply. Like a crime syndicate, Anderson's family of bad actors all speak the same 'language,' and all accept extreme behavior as normal, even routine. Some critics see too much of Scorsese's shadow falling over the film's visual style, but in truth Anderson's voice is quite distinct from Scorsese's; placing a much greater emphasis on emotional relationships. Particularly in the arena of romantic love, Anderson displays a sincerity and compassion often lacking in Scorsese's pictures. Very rarely does Scorsese allow his major characters to pursue, let alone attain, requited love. By contrast, the redemptive power of love runs strongly throughout Anderson's canon; especially in his earlier films. It's also worth remembering that Anderson is himself a well-informed filmmaker — one whose influences extend beyond Scorsese to include Altman, Ophuls, Kubrick, Demme, Melville, and a host of others.

Of course, the most direct inspiration for 'Boogie Nights' comes from Anderson himself. His first short film, 'The Dirk Diggler Story' forms the basis for this greatly enlarged offering; here multiplying the original 31-minute story several times over. On top of that, he enriches the narrative with a wealth of peripheral characters and subplots, many of which radically alter the pessimistic tone of that earlier film. 'Boogie Nights' presents a surprisingly affectionate story; one that knocks its characters around for much of the film, yet delivers them into a modest happiness by the end. Particularly distinct, when compared to 'The Dirk Diggler Story,' is the fate of Dirk himself, who avoids the fatal penalty imposed upon him in that earlier work.

It is perhaps through the film's peripheral characters that Anderson shows himself to be a more mature artist. As noted earlier, an aesthetic cynicism runs strongly through his experimental short-films—yet this cynicism seems fully exorcised by the time he enters his major phase of filmmaking. Here, in 'Boogie Nights,' he not only finds a life worth living for Dirk, he makes room for requited love, forgiveness, redemption, and a warmth of interpersonal relationship absent in his early work. The generosity he extends to his characters, allowing each of them to work through their struggles to find a sense of solace, emanates from an artist whose portrayal of humanity had grown exponentially by this point in time. Anderson constructs a narrative that again sees the value in unique relationships formed between flawed gods and lost men; everyday people whose moral compass sits a little off-center. On a larger scale, it is again the theme of divine intervention which brings these characters into one another's orbit, and sets them moving toward hardship and absolution.

A standard interpretation of 'Boogie Nights' might focus on the film's chronological transition from one decade to the next. In this interpretation, the film represents the passing of a golden era of creativity, brought to ruin by the onset of a less special era of calculated enterprise. To be sure,

Anderson's naïve characters are thrust from the 70's into the 80's without warning; forced to forego their earthly paradise for a less happy purgatory. Anderson's implied disdain for this sudden transition (as evinced in the film) can be extrapolated to represent a disdain for any number of cultural transitions which obliterate an earlier period's unique mode of expression. For example, 'Boogie Nights' can be seen as representative of the transition from Hollywood movie-making in the 80's to Independent filmmaking in the 90's. A movement from lavish blockbusters to the gradual employment of less expensive digital video—allowing nearly anyone to make their own movies and market them. This interpretation is useful, but it is secondary to appreciating the film in relation to Anderson's evolution as an artist. Moving from the simplicity of 'The Dirk Diggler Story' to the panorama of 'Boogie Nights,' one can barely grasp the notion that the latter emerged from the former.

*

'Electricity' is the word that best describes the opening of the film. Anderson takes the viewer on a tour of the San Fernando Valley circa 1977, diving headfirst into Maurice's swanky nightclub to introduce a plethora of ecstatic characters (while the Emotions' 'Best of My Love' blares happily in the background). These shots convey joyful movement; a sense of careening through a fantastic place and time. Rollergirl, Reed Rothchild, Buck Swope, Amber Waves—the viewer meets them all in the most vital manner, each more fascinating than the last; a testament to Anderson's instinct for crafting characters of enormous life and likability. The steadicam which acts as our virtuoso tour-guide then settles on the lone figure of Eddie Adams. Eddie from Torrance, soon to be transformed into the much larger-than-life Dirk Diggler.

Here, in this pivotal moment, the hand of divine providence descends from above to deliver Eddie into the arms of Jack Horner, expertly rendered by Burt Reynolds. Eddie is a simple dishwasher—a man whose one claim to fame is a lengthy piece of anatomy too often hidden from the public. By all appearances, this young man is not destined to acquire any fame or fortune. His character is marked by deep immaturity and a lack of ambition that show him incapable of being the architect of his own promotion. Words come slowly to him; and his body-language conveys emotional uncertainty. The fact that he's a high-school dropout who travels by bus to work does nothing to enhance his qualifications.

But Jack Horner is Eddie's guardian angel, conceived by P.T. Anderson to shepherd this everyday laborer into a greater world. Neither Jack nor Eddie knows it yet, but these two are (literally) made for each other. To bridge the gap between them, Anderson again utilizes the framework of divine intervention to bring one character into the sphere of another—not unlike the moment when Sydney invites John into the coffee-shop in 'Hard Eight.' This vehicle for relationship-building, so prominent in Anderson's art, cannot simply be dismissed as a cinematic device. Rather, it's a very deliberate method of translating human motive into drama. In Anderson's hands, this usually proceeds to a purposeful dynamic built around an imbalance of power. Here, one man (Jack) possess it, and another man (Eddie) doesn't. Jack draws Eddie into his world, and maintains a strong paternal influence over him.

At the same time — and this is a nod to Anderson's skill as a writer — Eddie draws Jack. The dynamic between them is conceived as a mutual exchange, each person hoping to gain something from the other (also reminiscent of the dynamic between John and Sydney). It's a compelling recipe for human theater, one which allows Anderson to enact his preference for revealing flawed figures. Eddie and Jack are not brought together by chance; instead the more powerful character descends to shepherd the less powerful into a more beautiful existence. The position Jack occupies in Eddie's life is best understood as that of father to son, or flawed god to lost man.

In 'Boogie Nights' this peculiar dynamic is accorded much greater weight than in Anderson's previous films. It's also extended for the first time to include an exploration of mother/daughter roles (as exemplified by Amber and Roller-girl) as well as the entire concept of 'family' itself. Of course Anderson's depiction of 'family' is often dysfunctional. That proves true here as well, both in the home-life of Eddie and in the various relationships that unfold as the movie progresses. It's worth noting that in telling the story of Eddie Adams (delicately conveyed by Mark Wahlberg) Anderson begins with the story of his family. Steeped in emotional trauma, Eddie's family is a nightmare. The young runaway is only too happy to find solace in the shelter Jack provides.

As noted earlier, Anderson's approach to the film is resoundingly uninhibited. The first confirmation of this occurs during the introductory scene between Jack and Eddie. Jack, sensing that Eddie is more than just a run-of-the-mill dishwasher, approaches him in the kitchen of Maurice's nightclub, and asks him a few simple questions. With no sense of shame or hesitation, Eddie then asks Jack if he wants the five-dollar deal or the ten. Jack is puzzled, and Eddie explains that if he wants to see his penis it's five dollars, but if he wants to watch Eddie masturbate, it's ten. The scene establishes a fearless approach to the subject-matter because it's played so straight. No affectation, no distorted camera-angles or wry music in the background; just a simple inquiry that leads to a straightforward offer. Anderson's dry sense of comedy rings true here, devising a dialogue so disarming that it confirms the reality of everyday figures living their lives without giving thought to the uncommon things they're discussing. No money changes hands and no deal is struck; but the chemistry between the two is immediately apparent. Without quite knowing it, Eddie has met his savior – the man who will lead him into the promised land. But not before Eddie lets go of his dysfunctional family.

Eddie returns to his room, where the walls display a wealth of iconic imagery: racing cars, bikini-clad starlets, feathered hair, concert superstars, and of course, the masterful Bruce Lee. This is Eddie the teenage dreamer, half the time enamored with his own image, half the time awash in youthful insecurity. The full-length mirror (a symbolic portal used throughout the film) reveals the idealized version of Eddie. In that polished glass his karate moves seem fantastic indeed. His attention fixates on his monstrous appendage – which he strokes adoringly, even protectively.

The music implies the optimism of youth; so crucial to understanding his peculiar character. Eddie's dreams can't be fulfilled through accepted social pathways, but he still believes he can make a name for himself somewhere.

Wahlberg imbues the character with genuine sympathy; sometimes quiet and vulnerable, sometimes overflowing with ambition. When morning comes, the scene shifts to the Adams' family kitchen. His apathetic father stands aside, totally detached from everything around him (including Eddie). But his mother is quite a different story. She towers over Eddie's subconscious; he feels worthless in her eyes. Like a natural predator she relishes her dominant position, preying on Eddie's insecurities if only to forget her loveless marriage. In contrast to the dazzle of Eddie's room, the layout of the kitchen is dreary. Fake wood-paneling, drab color, and dull plastic pieces signal gloom and mediocrity. Eddie knows he must escape this fabricated world or be smothered by it. Here Anderson heightens our sense of investment in the character, suggesting his woeful fate if he remains tethered to these strange and defeated people.

Thus, Anderson gives Eddie a viable alternative. He returns us to Jack's world, and introduces a gallery of potent (and impotent) players. William H. Macy plays the pitiful Little Bill, forever intruding on the sexual escapades of his wife (Nina Hartley). Julianne Moore portrays Amber Waves, the unfit mother to a child she's never allowed to see. Heather Graham is the heavenly Rollergirl, forever fed-up with the infantile theater of high school.

Don Cheadle is the soul of the film: the affectionately off-kilter Buck Swope. His character is special because he represents the vessel through which Anderson communicates his vision of romantic love, and the inexplicable way it often flowers. In nearly all of his movies, somewhere amid the mire, Anderson allows this fruitful flower to blossom. His star-crossed lovers symbolize the small hope at the bottom of Pandora's Box; they are the light of his films. In 'Boogie Nights' it's the luminous relationship between Buck and Jessie that exemplify the director's faith in humanity—so different from the pessimism surrounding 'The Dirk Diggler Story.'

Eddie's final exodus from home—banishment really—triggers the emotional break from his natural family. That break is paramount because Anderson's narrative demands an emotional investment in Eddie's life away from home. If there's any sense that Eddie's family-life is overflowing with love and support, much of Anderson's experiment would implode. We would not believe in Eddie's 'need' to belong to a surrogate family, which in turn would make his actions seem hollow. But Anderson is cunning. He fashions a plausible escape for Eddie; away from his personal inferno and into the paradise which awaits.

The confrontational scene between Eddie and his mother hits with raw intensity. Even though her temper has been shown in previous scenes, the sheer derision she levels at her son catches him completely off-guard. He arrives home very late, after meeting with Jack, Amber, and Rollergirl, to find his mother waiting in darkness. Seething with malice she zeroes in on his insecurity, ramping up the voltage by denouncing him as a loser. She displays a monstrous power here, moving with impressive tenacity. In his meager defense, Eddie can only beg: "Please don't be mean to me!" He erupts in a burst of hurt emotion, pushing her against the wall. She remains unmoved by his physical weakness and convinced of his stupidity. The damage is irreversible. Eddie flees the false-sanctuary of his home, and never looks back.

*

Of course, the film's architecture depends on Eddie finding a new home, a place where he legitimately — even spiritually — fits in; a world that not only appreciates his talent but celebrates it in an emotionally validating manner. He thus invests himself completely in Jack's new family; so much so that his tragic home-life seems a bad dream from which he's finally awakened. The early scenes at Jack's sensational compound are indeed symbolic of Eddie's new life — his baptism into an earthly paradise, complete with ceremonial pool. It's entirely appropriate that Elvin Bishop's 'Fooled Around and Fell In Love' plays as he dives into the christening waters; the moment highlighted by Anderson's judiciously timed slow-motion. Eddie from Torrance is born again in this brave new world.

The entire sequence unfolds as an overture to a golden age. Anderson's camera wanders through a veritable Garden of Eden, filling in the outlines of his previous character-sketches. Here, Buck Swope and his clueless fashion choices; there, Little Bill trying to scuttle yet another public penetration of his wife. Finally, the Colonel; a big-boned producer who bankrolls Jack's pornographic enterprise. "It's an important part of the process," Jack tells Eddie. Circling the pool on all sides is an endless throng of makeshift stars and starlets; whether it's Reed Rothchild mixing high-voltage margaritas or everyone's favorite sidekick, Scotty. He too merits honorable mention as the small fish in a big pond – the one figure in the film who loves Eddie unconditionally. Normally this kind of character would be a mere side-dish, but so sensitive is Anderson's palate, and so flavorful is Philip Seymour Hoffman's portrayal, that he seems to satisfy every appetite. He loves Eddie more than he loves himself, reminding the audience just how special Eddie – so close to stardom – really is.

It's at the end of this long baptismal scene, set in a pool of cleansing water, that Jack's new disciple is given a proper name. Gently swaying in the warmth of a hot tub, Eddie, Jack, and Reed form a symbolic holy trinity. In this pregnant moment Eddie becomes reborn as Dirk Diggler. "I want a name that can cut glass!" he declares. And indeed the naming process is a poetic ode to the new birth he experiences in Paradise, forever relinquishing his former identity. It's an immaculate conception, and Jack is pleased: "I think Heaven has sent you here, Dirk Diggler. I think the angels have blessed us all because of you." Reed concludes the prayer with a single word: "Amen." This moment is crucial to understanding the impulse of Anderson's art. The symbolism is biblical. It is divine intervention that delivers Eddie unto Jack. His baptism, rebirth, reign of glory, and fall from grace are all fashioned as a modern parable. Dirk Diggler will inevitably succumb to the sin of Pride, doomed to lose his way in the world even after receiving everything he desired. But not just yet.

The intoxicating reign of king Dirk, while it lasts, is a supreme achievement in Anderson's canon. In no other film is any character accorded so much success in so short a time, so free of negative consequence. His rise to stardom comes faster than even Daniel Plainview's in 'There Will Be Blood,' and it's unhampered by the emotional difficulties that destroy Daniel's personal relationships. Comparing Dirk to Barry Egan in 'Punch Drunk Love,' his success is more celebrated; and comparing him to Sydney, his level of 'spiritual' gratification is unblemished. Sydney harbored a past that darkened even his most rewarding moments—in fact, they motivated those moments—but so complete is Dirk's transformation that Eddie Adams seems never to have existed in the first place. And perhaps because 'Magnolia' spreads itself across so massive a canvas, none of its characters can match the focused supremacy of Dirk Diggler—not even T.J. Mackie, whose success must always be weighed against a deep fund of emotional damage. No, Dirk stands tallest amid Anderson's kingdom; and the director allows him to flare— however briefly—like a big, bright, shining star.

The first 'acting' scene between Dirk and Amber is a richly perverse example of Anderson's wry humor, as he affectionately recreates the awful dialogue and threadbare plot of 70's era pornography. That Mark Wahlberg and Julianne Moore deliver these lines with such conviction only confirms Anderson's sure grasp of this absurd social enclave. His ability to balance imagery that is both erotic and amusing reveals an intuitive sense of restraint. A lesser director would've jumped at the chance to display full-frontal nudity amid hardcore drama. But Anderson is more interested in sculpting selective images that introduce the viewer to this world without exploiting it. By doing so he keeps the focus on the human side of the story. His conscious decision not to display Dirk's enormous appendage is akin to Spielberg's careful timing in 'Jaws;' keeping the shark a mystery until the weight of the film builds it into a genuine monster.

This is a heady time for Dirk, fully symbolic of man's carefree existence in the Garden of Eden. Everyone who partakes of this paradise is rewarded with a hedonistic level of euphoria and happiness, and everyone bestows upon Dirk the highest accolade for elevating their world into a place of harmony. Now, some argue that this celebratory treatment of Dirk's profession is little more than a glamorization of pornography. But if this was Anderson's intent, he could have easily ended the film prior to thrusting his characters headfirst into the 1980's. In the last half of the film he allows his characters to fall completely from grace, sending them on self-destructive journeys through their own personal infernos. The glorious ecstasy that Anderson celebrates in the first half of the film is matched measure-for-measure by personal humiliation and absence of success in the second.

It's worth repeating that much of Anderson's aesthetic sensibility derives from thematic material derived from the Old Testament—not literally, but rather on a level that considers the timeless truths of its human drama. In none of his films are any characters allowed easy access to personal solace or spiritual satisfaction. Rather, Anderson's sensibility demands suffering. The protagonist must earn his sense of meaningful achievement. That is true here, as it is in all of his films. Dirk Diggler's early success is not permanent. He will fall from grace, and lose everything he owns (including himself) before being allowed absolution. It's this very aspect of Anderson's art—his keen understanding of human odyssey — that makes his cinema so durable and rewarding. At its core are the most arduous human trials.

In the meantime, Jack continues to shepherd his flock through a sexual wonderland. Much of the film's sheer energy derives from a wealth of enthusiastic performances, especially those of John C. Riley, Mark Wahlberg, and Don Cheadle. Their dialogue is a melting pot of youthful musings, reminding us that for all their celebrity, they're basically just kids. Especially Dirk and Rollergirl, whose dialogue is refreshingly direct: "Do you like these shoes? They're Italian. Yeah, they're really cool!" Anderson's vigor is equally refreshing, spinning a flurry of images ranging from Dirk's moves on the dance floor to the pornographic films-within-a-film that never cease to amuse. This is joyful momentum, conveyed with great skill through Anderson's precocious mastery of the camera.

It is through the introduction of Jessie (played with great sincerity by Melora Walters) that Buck Swope's aesthetic importance to the film becomes evident. Her first appearance does not imply anything more than a peripheral role, but this subtlety allows the romantic core of their story to blossom in a manner that does not overwhelm the narrative. Her disarming lack of agenda, and natural sweetness, make her the perfect harbor for Buck's aimless direction. The joke that runs through the first half of the film, lampooning Buck's struggle to find the right 'look,' evaporates when Jesse sits beside him at a New Years Eve party. Buck, having cloaked himself in yet another fashion disaster, finally decides enough is enough. In a moment of rare honesty, he takes off his wig and plops it on the table. But instead of laughing at him, as so many have done, Jessie laughs with him. It suddenly becomes obvious that *she* is the right fit for Buck. Their sincere dialogue, shifting from a love of sunsets to Buck's dream of selling hi-fidelity stereos at discount prices, is the expression of two people discovering a true love for one another. For Anderson these moments incarnate the redemptive power of requited love, so crucial to his art. The mode of romanticism he favors is subtle, tailored to a quiet faith in humanity that again supersedes the artist's more pessimistic early phase of filmmaking.

Of course, Jack stands at the center of it all; the ringmaster of a bloated circus. He too will fall victim to the rapidly changing world around him; unwilling to accept those changes until they overwhelm him completely. Even his crowning achievement, the Chest Rockwell series of films, is not enough to lift him above the shifting tide. The decade to come, the 1980's, will bring great storm and stress to these naïve figures—and Anderson, quite literally, ushers it in with a bang.

The New Years Eve party which marks the end of an era begins without any special fanfare. Some of the scenery has changed, and one key player has been added. Todd Parker enters the picture, signaling the start of a rapid descent for Dirk and Reed. He's an figurative demon who takes these young protagonists down to the underworld. He's out of place in this paradise—an intruder whose presence is unfortunately necessary. Like a virus he's settled into an open sore; his arrival portends disease and decay. Similarly unsettling is the humiliation experienced by Scotty in the aftermath of kissing Dirk on the mouth. Dirk, of course, recoils in disgust, leaving Scotty to wallow in his own private misery behind the wheel of his car, drowning himself in the same repeated mantra: "I'm a fucking idiot!" A darkness descends over this once sunny paradise.

Back inside, events spin out of control. An unacknowledged change is occurring. The center cannot hold. Finally Anderson sends in the ultimate symbol of bottled rage: William H. Macy's Little Bill. This figure single-handedly symbolizes the self-destruction of an era. His violent actions summon the specter of death and introduce a severity of tone nowhere to be found in the first half of the film.

The scene opens on a steadicam shot following him into the house as he seeks his wayward wife. As he nears the bedroom, partygoers race back and forth, eager for the countdown to midnight. As Bill enters the bedroom he witnesses an image he's seen one too many times: another man in bed with his wife. Everyone has his breaking point, and this is Little Bill's. He retraces his steps outside and calmly grabs a revolver from the glove-box of his car. As the crowd mindlessly chants the countdown to midnight, he walks into the bedroom and blasts his wife and lover full of vengeful lead. The crowd senses something out of place. Bill emerges, no longer burdened by the diminutive prefix 'Little,' and turns the murderous weapon on himself. That act of final will, from a character previously devoid of will, catapults the film into a very different reality. No longer a blissful safe-haven, Jack's house is torn apart by a bolt of lightning from a wrathful god. It is a house divided; and more than any other family-member, it is Dirk who will suffer the greatest loss.

80's

The new decade opens on Amber's documentary of Dirk. The color is drab, the characters are bloated, and the enthusiasm is gone. The subjects look as if they just finished digging their own graves; one step from total collapse. Already in this little documentary Anderson is dismantling his characters' egos. Even Jack Horner has been marginalized. Video has displaced his beloved film as the medium of choice for pornography, sinking his dream of becoming a 'real filmmaker.' Everywhere the cracks are starting to show. This extended family, inseparable and incestuous, has been together too long. Earlier in the film their unity stemmed from genuine love; now they've become weary roommates crammed in a tiny apartment, unable to figure a way out of their dull morass.

In Amber's documentary, Reed's complexion resembles winter ash. Jittery, unpredictable gestures punctuate a diatribe of wild ambitions. Dirk too seems unbalanced and agitated. The world has changed too rapidly for these unprepared figures. They cannot adapt to new roles or reconceived boundaries. To compensate they take refuge in hard drugs, deluding themselves into believing the world will adjust to their mindless desires.

One by one, we witness the fall of once mighty figures. Even as the Colonel is jailed for molesting a child — disowned by Jack in his hour of need — the new kid on the block, Johnny Doe, topples Dirk from his pornographic throne. This young stud is brought into the business because he understands the rapid turnaround required for the industry. VHS is the new medium, and mail-order is the name of the game. Jack needs hard workers to make the magic happen, and unfortunately Dirk appears more impotent every day.

In one particularly humiliating scene, he fails to summon the arousal needed for one of Jack's movies; a task that was once laughably easy. But Dirk is weary, stressed, and pumped full of drugs. He becomes enraged, confronting his guardian angel face-to-face. The ensuing rupture between Jack and Dirk, father and son, flawed god and lost man, is devastating to witness. Dirk demands to shoot the scene and Jack refuses, exclaiming: "You're fired! Get the fuck outta here!" To which Dirk replies: "I'm the biggest star here! I wanna fuck, it's my big dick, everybody get ready fuckin' now! You know what? I don't need this shit! You're not the king of me! You're NOTHING without me, Jack!" With that, he is once again exiled from home; a devastating repetition of the earlier banishment he suffered at the hands of his wrathful mother.

Dirk descends into the lower rings of a figurative hell. He and Reed attempt to conquer the world of pop-music, believing it to be no different than conquering porn. The pop-lyrics Anderson forces Dirk to sing are pure agony, but they're magnificent too in nailing down the overblown ballads of the era: "You're a WIN-ner! You're NO-body's fool!" Dirk stumbles through the notes at full volume, absolutely enthralled by his own star-power. He drags Reed with him into this realm of delusion, further and further down, fueling their miserable journey with a heady combination of drugs and hubris. At this point, no character escapes Dirk's curse. He brings failure to everything he touches.

Meanwhile Amber and Rollergirl develop a perverse mother/daughter relationship, ironically built around Amber's willful adoption of the young starlet even as she's barred from seeing her own biological son. Amber's years of sexual deviance and drug abuse have deprived her of any legitimate claim to motherhood, so she resorts to being Rollergirl's make-believe mom. It's a painful instance of characters constructing an imaginary world that supersedes reality — eagerly believing the emotional fulfillment they long for is sated by their actions.

Anderson fires on all cylinders in this difficult phase of the film, cutting with rapid-fire precision, careening from one grotesque scene to the next, maintaining a breathless pace that evokes the nausea of near-vomiting. He animates a world of easy drugs, sexual dysfunction, and clueless decision. None of these characters knows what they're doing or who they are; they just keep stumbling further into the abyss. It's a spectacular fall from grace — and proof-positive that Anderson never once envisioned their previous paradise as a place of permanent residence. These characters must suffer individually and collectively on their long journey to redemption. This middle-point of the narrative is a consistently dark marker in Anderson's cinema. It's just around this point that the fates of his characters turn 180 degrees from their prior good fortune.

And then there's Buck Swope. This shy figure, so wrong about everything in the 70's, suddenly finds himself on a path to personal success. He's the reverse-image of all the figures around him. When they were on top of the world he struggled to find a place for himself, always off-center. Now with everyone at the bottom he begins a most peculiar climb to the top. Modest, loving, and devoted to his new wife Jessie, he applies for a loan to fund his dreams. Sadly, the world is still a harsh place. The bank denies this young couple for one simple reason: "We cannot endorse pornography!" But Anderson will not refuse these characters their happiness. He's carved a special niche for these two; they represent his faith in redemptive love. As such they will not be subjected to the same inferno reserved for his principal characters. Buck and Jessie don't get their loan, but a saving grace — a gift from above — awaits them both.

Back at the warehouse Jack Horner wanders through a maze of shipping crates; the vassal of a video empire. He was once a man of talent; a genuine film director. Now his world is very different and much less special. As Kurt (his video editor) describes their most recent project: "It is what it is." But the sequence which truly represents the low-point of the film doesn't begin until Jack sets out to make "film history on video tape." Anderson constructs a narrative parallel between two scenes which juxtaposes an instance of deep humiliation for Jack and Rollergirl with an instance of brutality and shame for Dirk. This is the lowest circle of their veritable hell, designed specifically to bury these characters under the weight of their own sinful pride.

The sequence opens on Jack and Rollergirl in a limousine, embarking on a cinematic experiment to find a man on the street who's willing to share a sex-scene with Rollergirl. Simultaneously, in another part of the city, Dirk wanders through town at midnight. Darkness reigns. Jack and Rollergirl manage to find a willing participant, and very soon they invite him into the car. Meanwhile a lone driver invites Dirk into his truck. He accepts. The score of the film becomes ominous and deathly — a tolling bell signals the blackest hour for these once proud characters. It quickly becomes apparent that the man-on-the-street knows Rollergirl — he even mentions her real name, Randi. Dirk's driver, on the other hand, has never even heard of him. He stops the truck and asks Dirk to masturbate for him. He replies: "Twenty bucks," to which the driver counters: "Ten's all I have." This parallel sequence strips away the very identities of the film's most celebrated characters. Rollergirl is reduced to Randi the high-school dropout; and Dirk regresses into Eddie Adams, once again masturbating for a stranger's money. It's a profoundly pitiful moment — especially since Dirk can't even manage an erection.

Rollergirl calls off the experiment after the man-on-the-street assails her with his bloated body. He harbors no respect for this once shimmering starlet, or for Jack either. As he's kicked out of the car he curses: "Your fuckin' films suck now anyway!" It's too much for Jack to handle; he tackles the man recklessly. But the real savagery comes when Rollergirl, the child who never stood up for herself, takes out a lifetime's worth of frustrations on this man who made her feel so worthless. "You don't ever disrespect me!" she cries. His head nearly comes apart under her jackhammer skates, even as Dirk, on the other end of town, is rudely surprised when the driver's friends arrive and pull him from the truck. They beat him into a red mess; a pile of waste writhing on the ground with his dumb pride between his legs. "You don't do this, donkey-dick!" the driver roars. And with that, they disappear into the night. Dirk cowers in the fetal position, totally humiliated. The entire scene is a mesmerizing portrait of degradation, and a physical reminder of life's bitter consequences. Here Anderson refuses to shy away from exposing raw vulnerability, insisting his characters become aware of the dark depths they've reached. But the arc of this sequence is not yet complete. These scenes merge into a revelatory example of his art—not for what they depict, but for what they introduce.

Artistically speaking, the nourishment of a small seed of hope from an instance of tragedy is intrinsic to Anderson's portrait of human optimism. The pure shame experienced by Dirk, Rollergirl, and Jack forms a moment of self-awareness in the film. These characters can sink no lower. Yet in the aftermath of these scenes, Anderson purposely shifts to the image of Buck's white Volvo driving into the parking lot of a donut shop. These silent ships passing in the night—the trucks making their getaway, Jack's limousine limping home, and Buck's Volvo—all captured in the same frame display Anderson's masterful grasp of composition. He moves seamlessly, miraculously, from personal shame and trauma to the greater benevolence of divine intervention. Buck and Jessie are not just vessels of romantic love, they're symbols of rebirth (as evidenced by Jessie's pregnant condition). In keeping with that theme, Anderson devises a quiet resurrection—a new life—for this faithful young couple.

The scene begins with wonderful normalcy: Buck browses through the shop, picking out a baker's dozen, while Jessie waits in the car. A midnight marauder enters the store with hostile intent. He pulls a gun and demands cash. Buck instantly freezes, unwilling to provoke the man, conscious of his wife and unborn son outside. Then a strange miracle occurs. A man sitting at a nearby booth draws a revolver and shoots the armed robber, whose gun fires twice, killing both the store-clerk and that same man at the booth. The bloodshed is over before it started. Three men are dead; but more importantly for Buck, a packed bag of loot is left on the floor. Buck stares at the blood, remembers the injustice done to him in the bank, and does what any dreamer would do: takes advantage of this gift from above.

This sequence, played with truthfulness and odd comedy, celebrates the mystery of divine providence. Throughout Anderson's films this powerful theme will recur again and again, consistently used to determine the fate of his most important characters. In 'Boogie Nights' it's Eddie Adams who find himself most affected on the largest scale. But on a smaller, more hopeful scale, it's Buck Swope. As the heart of the film, he seeks—and finds—a light at the end of the tunnel. Anderson grants him that pathway in a sequence that again calls to mind a Pandora's Box. Emerging from the previous scene's darkness and misery, Buck (appropriately dressed in white) becomes a quiet beacon of optimism. That this incident occurs just before Christmas Day only highlights the halo of divinity surrounding this special scene.

Long Way Down (one last thing)

In the last act of the film Anderson moves toward resolution. Because Dirk has fallen so far, so fast, only an extreme experience can provide him a moment of true awakening. This is well in keeping with his character; defined as it is by behavior at the edge of societal norms. Thus Anderson fashions for him a near-death experience, one that violently brings Dirk face-to-face with his own mortality. Todd Parker, the dark figure who represents temptation in the film, concocts a plan to score some fast cash from a drug-dealer named Rahad. He convinces Dirk and Reed to join him. Their ludicrous scheme (involving the sale of fake drugs) is the ultimate example of cluelessness when it comes to comprehending the world beyond pornography. They have no idea what lies outside their little enclave, and haven't the ability to manage the unexpected.

Dirk and Reed follow Todd blindly. They arrive at the dealer's house, and discover (much to their surprise) that Todd packs a gun. They soon notice that Rahad's bodyguard is also armed. Tensions rise, and the threat of sudden danger becomes very real. Dirk and Reed begin to panic even as Todd plows ahead with his naïve scheme. Anderson floods the scene with adrenaline, shaping Rahad into a spontaneous madman. He loves his mix-tapes, his cabin-boy, and the thrill of bursting firecrackers. This last device punctuates every gesture with visceral potency, foreshadowing the gunfire to come. Every sight and sound seems heightened out of proportion to the characters' abilities; and the accelerating sense of threat breeds a palpable anxiety. In this inescapable situation Anderson brings the entire film to a moment of extreme awareness.

Todd announces his purpose, and chaos ensues. He and the bodyguard draw their guns, and bullets roar. Rahad, astonished that these half-wits intended to rob him, scurries to his bedroom, while the scene careens into manic insanity. Dirk and Reed scatter behind the bar, desperate to escape. Todd is dead, the bodyguard is dead, and Rahad suddenly appears with a 12-gauge shotgun, blasting holes in every wall. The clamor is deafening. Dirk somehow makes it outside, jumps into his car, and floors the accelerator—even as a gun-blast annihilates his window. Reed makes it out too, albeit on foot, scrambling like a lunatic. Finally Dirk is left alone to reflect on his folly. His emotional release is deep and despairing, laden with emptiness. Symbolically, his beloved Corvette runs out of gas.

But Anderson provides him one final instance of divine intervention. Dirk finds himself exactly where he started: the safe-haven of Jack Horner's earthly paradise; his symbol of emotional shelter. Jack's home becomes the setting for a spiritual reunion, embodying both forgiveness and redemption. Eddie humbly enters with nothing but the shirt on his back, just as he did all those years ago, and apologizes with sincere humility. Jack, of course, takes him back into his arms; the flawed god reclaiming his prodigal son. This shared moment draws the film back to its point of origin, signaling the renewal of a special relationship here more meaningful by virtue of each character's long odyssey home. The theme of 'home' is another constant in Anderson's cinema. Time and again his most special characters are brought symbolically home after their arduous journeys. It is the harbor of personal solace, manifested purposely and unapologetically.

The world for Jack and Dirk is very different now, and each of them must make their life anew. The collective journey they've taken is summed up by acceptance, absolution, and adaptation. The film's characters are no longer the same people they once were, and Anderson charitably grants them a chance to succeed through new endeavors. Amber's venture as a film-director parallels her closer relationship to Jack; Buck's stereo discount store complements his newborn baby; Reed's affectionate magic act coincides with Rollergirl's return to high school. All of these efforts reveal a collective growth of character. The choice of music, Brian Wilson's immaculate 'God Only Knows What I'd Be Without You' captures the warm-hearted tone Anderson strikes for this diminished paradise. His characters have endured heaven and hell; and in the end have come to appreciate a more earthbound sense of happiness. A human halo surrounds their new lives together, fostering a mellow sense of optimism.

Dirk's new life is more complicated. Anderson still grants his protagonist a certain generosity — especially compared to the fatal outcome that befell the earlier figure in 'The Dirk Diggler Story.' Yet here, despite new life, Dirk's redemption is tempered. Indeed, in many ways he's the figure who matures the least. Dirk reclaims his credentials as a pornography actor, but does not seem to gain a wisdom comparable to the struggle he's endured.

Anderson constructs the final scene, literally, as a personal reflection. Alone in his dressing room, Dirk stares into the mirror, still fascinated by himself and his body. As before, the mirror represents a portal—the only vessel through which Dirk assesses himself. He likes what he sees. He understands his place in the world and the very special gift he brings to it. Right on cue, he pulls his pants down— even as his face moves entirely out of frame. One is substituted for the other; and shrewdly, deliberately, this mirror-image is the only prism through which Anderson allows Dirk's penis to be seen.

In that reflection Dirk observes the only thing that ever validated his existence: his larger-than-life appendage. It's a bittersweet epilogue, for Anderson portrays a man who can't adapt to a changing world and hasn't matured despite his suffering. Instead he still hides behind his only asset; a massively proportioned crutch that renders Dirk (the man) insignificant by comparison.

Symbolically, his desire for the fame he once enjoyed is an attempt to reenter the Garden of Eden before the Fall— before the great expulsion from paradise. Anderson's mirrored portrait of Dirk is painfully regressive; a one-dimensional profile of a man who invests his real self in the reflection he sees. As before with Amber and Rollergirl, this is an instance of a character imagining a world greater than reality. All Dirk's best days are behind him (a sad reflection), and his present desire is only to recreate the past. It's a heartbreaking incarnation of man's fallen state, instantly foreshadowing the words of Jimmy Gator in Anderson's next film, 'Magnolia': "The Book says we might be through with the past, but that past ain't through with us." It is a fitting and poignant end to a narrative rooted in biblical parable.

In the final shot, Anderson draws the curtain. He symbolizes Dirk's shallow desire to relive his glory-years by looking backward through cinematic reference. Within this dressing-room image, Mark Wahlberg is Eddie Adams as Dirk Diggler recreating Robert DeNiro as Jake Lamotta recreating Marlon Brando as Terry Malloy musing silently: "I could've been somebody." The receding image suggests a faded reproduction: a copy of a copy of a copy through which Dirk longs to reproduce his rapid rise to stardom. The last words of the film are then magnificently ironic. Eddie Adams utters aloud the mantra that only he believes, himself become a flawed god:

"I am a big bright shining star."

Part Three:

MAGNOLIA

*

Of all P.T. Anderson's films to this point, 'Magnolia' is undoubtedly the most ambitious. It's the film that displays the greatest variety of character and the most abstract presentation of symbol. The flower from which the title takes its name is primarily associated with nobility, love, and perseverance; themes which Anderson buries deep in the film's body. This is an intensely personal film; one made up of solemnity, discovery, and emotional closure. It is also electrifying, and funny. The variety of truths that emerge over the course of the film, and how those truths affect a myriad of damaged figures, forms the narrative foundation. Their quest to find some semblance of peace, some inner-light, moves the film forward. Anderson guides the viewer through this traumatic gathering with unerring direction. For him 'Magnolia' represents a personal flowering—both in the content of the film and its seamless execution. In no previous effort is his artistry communicated with such perceptive depth. That he places his talent at the service of a narrative devoted to dignity, love, and truth, only confirms his generosity as a filmmaker.

'Magnolia' is also the film which opens itself to the widest variety of interpretation; not because of its length (at three solid hours his longest film), but by virtue of the fact that Anderson spreads his artistic acumen over so broad a canvas. The gallery of major players here is immense, nearly overwhelming the action with individual personalities that each require equal consideration. And because his characters don't always share a physical connection to one another, their individual predicaments become all the more crucial to discerning a common motif. Because Jimmy Gator does not know Frank T.J. Mackie, who does not know Officer Jim, who does not know Stanley Spector, etc., an interpretation of the film based on direct relationships does not suffice. Rather, these characters must be understood by examining the emotional proximity they share. In this regard, Anderson assigns each of them a devastating (if unifying) quota of personal loss and misfortune. For some characters this misfortune is self-inflicted (i.e. 'Quiz Kid' Donnie Smith). The majority, however, are depicted as victims of chance, or fate, which Anderson unapologetically threads into their lives like a deadly web.

Another challenge is posed by the film's sophisticated progression of theme. Anderson sets up a cunning ruse at the outset meant to emphasize the secular notion of coincidence. He portrays a rapid sequence of unrelated encounters meant to set the stage for the action to follow. This masterful opening — so very like an operatic overture — is a jewel of rare brilliance and craftsmanship, linking a sequence of astonishing tales not by the characters in them, but rather by theme. Indeed, there is no relationship between the casino dealer who inadvertently dies at the hands of his patron; the young man whose suicide becomes a homicide; and the man killed by three robbers whose names match that of their victim's residence. Instead, the shared commodity here is the improbable circumstances surrounding their fates. Anderson dazzles the viewer with locomotive images, each cleverly imparting just enough information to match the narrator's emphasis on coincidence. Tragic coincidence to be more specific, for each of these victims meets an untimely death in this remarkable opening. Anderson masks that unifying theme of death (which becomes crucial to understanding the film's thematic progression) behind a barrage of sights and sounds constructed of such artistry that it goes almost unnoticed.

But the motif of death which sets the film in motion is actually an artful decoy. Indeed it's an irony given that only one character (Earl Partridge) dies in the body of the film proper—and that death is a repudiation of the notion that life and death are meaningless coincidences. Through Earl's death, and his dying words, Anderson affirms the individual meaning of life. He further asserts that death can be a bridge to personal resurrection. In fact, the film's ultimate denial of death is intrinsic to many of the characters' narrative arcs. For example, Linda Partridge and Jimmy Gator do not succeed in taking their own lives, despite their repeated efforts to do so. Again, this affirmation of life counters the film's murderous opening.

Instead, the long odyssey between the film's beginning and end is an artistic progression away from an emphasis on random chance to another sphere of coincidental momentum. That distinct incarnation of fate which Anderson associates with life rather than death is divine intervention. In this film, more so than any other, Anderson's allegiance to divinity is most powerfully communicated via symbol; specifically the fantastic rain of frogs that forms the climax of the film. It is this ambitious symbol which represents the summation of Anderson's art to this point; and it is the portal through which his characters are each delivered to some personal affirmation or emotional closure.

*

As the overture gives way to the body of the film, the first of Aimee Mann's melancholy songs—'One is the Loneliest Number'—marks the transition. It sets the film's emotional tone, underscoring the loneliness of disaffected figures even in the midst of family. As with 'Boogie Nights,' Anderson immediately introduces a wealth of characters, each of whom exist on a different physical plane yet share the same emotional distress. Here the variety of ensemble is stretched to the limit, elongating Anderson's art yet never causing the framework to collapse. It is the emotional unity between characters—their shared sense of trauma—that girds the film's architecture. For all his bravado, Frank T.J. Mackie is not so different from Stanley Spector, nor he from Claudia Gator; all of whom dwell in the shadow of paternal failure. Indeed, all of Anderson's characters are emotionally fractured, and all require individual moments of truth to realize some sense of personal solace. Perhaps the character most afflicted is Earl Partridge, patriarch of the Partridge family. His remorse is literally cancerous, and at the end of the film it is his death which represents a transformation from one state of being to another — from dark to light.

Filling in the picture are Earl's wife, Linda, terrified that her husband will soon leave her for the afterlife; Jimmy Gator, the weary game show host whose every minute on earth feels like a minute past his due; 'Quiz-Kid' Donnie Smith, whose unrequited love for a young bartender determines the bulk of his confused actions; Phil Parma, ever selfless, who devotes himself to Earl's final hours on Earth; and last but not least, Officer Jim Kurring, who occupies a special place in the film. Like Buck Swope in 'Boogie Nights,' this figure represents Anderson's vessel for conveying the redemptive power of love. His hopeful journey through a world of secrets and lies delivers him to the home of Claudia Wilson; itself a manifestation of divine providence.

Early in the film, Jim is introduced through a series of images set to his own narration for a dating-service: "I'm really interested in meeting someone special who likes quiet things. My life is very stressful. I hope to have a relationship that is very calm, and undemanding, and loving." This is an example of Anderson's ironic portrait of fate versus will. Jim willfully employs a dating-service to help him find the right woman. But his meeting with Claudia comes as an act absent of will, set into motion by divine providence. The symbol which most clearly weds him to religious iconography is the cross he kneels before in the introduction; another instance of Anderson's desire to imbue his favorite characters with a soul.

The world Anderson creates in 'Magnolia' is a labyrinth of miracle and mystery. It is also keenly structured as a progression of ideas. The first of these ideas — chance and coincidence—manifest themselves in the opening sequence; but over the course of the film Anderson gradually bends these ideas into a purposeful shape. The movie begins with a secular overture which proclaims the random nature of life and death. But as it gathers momentum, 'Magnolia' proceeds decisively away from the hopelessness of death to a more optimistic place of personal affirmation.

What accounts for this transition? Is it Anderson's effort to construct a narrative that turns from dark to light? Partly. But more specifically it's an artistic denunciation of aimless fate and secular coincidence. His thematic progression is intended to overturn the notion (outlined in the film's opening) that random chance renders life meaningless. Instead, Anderson's film argues that life is meaningful, even in the aftermath of death. This model shapes death into a resurrecting force, one that ultimately serves the living. It signals a passing from one state of being to another. In the body of the film, Anderson gives no validity to notions of random coincidence—rather everything happens for a reason. 'Magnolia,' of all Anderson's films, most forcefully advocates a faith in divine guidance and human regeneration. It further underscores his refusal to allow personal tragedies—even death—to defeat individual perseverance. This progression of ideas, from the hopelessness of random activity to the healing design of divine guidance—marks a new level of artistic sophistication in Anderson's cinema. For this reason, 'Magnolia' should be understood as a pivotal moment in his development as a filmmaker.

The great rain of frogs which forms the apex of the film, the summation of his ideas, proves through its very abstraction that secular fate—meaning fate that has no root in divine force — cannot explain a world capable of hope and love. It is the sheer impossibility of this terrifying storm that awakens each character from blind misfortune to a renewed sense of personal direction. The apocalyptic scale of the event buries petty notions of random coincidence; it renders them insignificant. The climax of the film is a massive, inexplicable, life-altering event that allows the film to take a profound leap of faith. That leap is transcendental; it provides a sense of hope that could not be realized given a simple belief in the randomness of life and death. Again, this is an unexpected progression given the film's deliberately haphazard opening. But as the narrative builds momentum, as personal conflicts come to a head, Anderson ensures that the hopelessness of coincidence is buried beneath a storm of biblical gravity.

Partly Cloudy, 82% Chance of Rain

Anderson's cleansing rain is foreshadowed by the first of his cinematic interludes, which anticipate the emotional tone of the scenes to follow. These interludes are simple weather descriptions, serving a purpose similar to the abstract color-segments in his next film, 'Punch Drunk Love.' From this point Anderson begins to fill in the outlines of his characters; first following Officer Jim into a blue-collar apartment where a routine disturbance becomes the scene of a murder. This sequence establishes his character, revealing him to be a dedicated officer committed to his profession;

which in turn helps define the subtle concepts of good and evil in the film.

From this scene Anderson pivots 180 degrees to spotlight Linda Partridge, wife of Earl; a figure consumed with anxiety. She confesses to her attorney that she shouldn't be included in her dying husband's will because she's cheated on him, stolen from him, and loathed him in the past. She doesn't deserve to benefit from his imminent death. Yet there's a deeper angst here, for Linda's true motive is fear — fear of living without her husband. This impending loneliness fosters a sudden 'love' for Earl, which in turn motivates her actions. In truth, Linda is a selfish creation whose manufactured love for Earl is rooted in a fear of living alone. She confuses love with dependence; becoming a tragic and pitiful figure in the process. She grasps at anything that might numb her feelings of emptiness, too terrified to face the world by herself. Anderson's writing here is highly nuanced, creating a multifaceted character who requires a layered approach to understanding her motives. Only at the end of the film, in her actions just prior to Earl's death, are those conflicting emotions mastered, allowing her a partial redemption.

Anderson, as an artist, sees difficulty in the world. His characters tend to come from unhappy places. They lack love, or solace, or a sense of belonging. But he also believes in hope, redemption, and humanity — all of which emerge through narrative conflict. Perhaps the two figures which best embody the distinction between these contrasting modes — cynicism and optimism — are Phil Parma and Earl Partridge. Their interaction calls to mind the chess-game between the young knight and the figure of Death in Ingmar Bergman's 'Seventh

Seal.' Here, Earl is the symbol of death, relentlessly disdaining life and lamenting his sinful past. His cynical view pollutes his soul as a cancer pollutes his body. Phil, on the other hand, is a marked contrast: the one entirely selfless creation in the film. He caters to Earl in a manner which suggests angelic patience. Earl views life as a sequence of lost opportunities, while Phil's great strength lies in his intuitive *grasp* of opportunity.

Upon hearing that Earl wishes to see his estranged son Frank Mackie, Phil imagines a reunion, even resolution, between these two disaffected figures. The effort which follows, as Phil overcomes every obstacle to finding the infamous Mackie, is a miraculous expression of Anderson's faith in human perseverance. Throughout the film he, Anderson, fashions a chessboard of moving pieces which form intricate patterns and connections, all converging on meaningful moments of personal truth.

Frank T.J. Mackie is one of the most extreme characters in any of Anderson's films. His psychology, derived from emotional pain and personal loss, spans an almost irreparable chasm. He can only find refuge behind a monstrous wall; a grotesque personality which drowns his past in a torrent of machismo. It's appropriate that his false-biography is only discovered under the scrutiny of a female journalist's interview, because he's a creature who cannot be honest with himself—his secret can only be revealed through the interrogation of another.

Mackie's defense-mechanisms block the trauma of childhood memories, seeking their annihilation through the invention of a new history. The result is a narrative suited to his emotional instability—an alternate reality in which his despised father is dead and his beloved mother is alive. In many ways he calls to mind the haunted figure of Norman Bates, keeping the memory of his dead mother alive even to the point that she influences his living motives. Unbeknownst to him, a rendezvous with divine intervention awaits — a call from beyond which finally reunites him with his father.

Tom Cruise's explosive performance as Mackie is the bravest in the film because it takes the greatest risk. Cruise portrays not just a loathsome figure, but one who is consistently validated for his repugnant behavior. He's a cult phenomenon who packages his emotional dysfunction and peddles it to the lonely and vulnerable. Mackie is both uncontainable and fearless; a vivid contrast to his father Earl who lays on his death-bed wallowing in regret. Of course Mackie hasn't reached that stage of personal reflection, so he thunders through the world atop his own massive ego. His moment of truth will not come until late in the film, at his father's bedside, where Mackie comes face to face with his personal demon.

The narrative turns from this relationship to that between Jimmy Gator and his daughter, Claudia. Early in the film it's made clear she wants nothing to do with her father, even as he attempts to bridge the gap between them. A crucial scene establishes their conflict. Jimmy enters her apartment in the aftermath of a one-night-stand. Claudia's body-language is defensive, vulnerable, and ashamed. She's a fragile vessel cracked in a million places struggling to keep herself together. Their confrontation displays Anderson's intuitive sense of drama, conjuring the faint specter of paternal judgment. Still, Jimmy makes an earnest attempt to reach her, but the pain is too deep. She cannot forgive him for his past abuse, even after he reveals to her that he's dying. "Get out! Get the fuck out of here!" she wails. Unlike Linda Partridge, Jimmy's motives are not based on a misreading of his feelings. He understands exactly what he's lost over the years, and his effort to repair the damage is genuine. His great failing is that he cannot confess his past sins — not even to himself — making him one of the many characters who assuage themselves through self-delusion.

Anderson's rendition of this fractured world, and the people in it, demands a high level of artistry. To nurture such a vast field of fallow emotions, make them grow and bear fruit, requires dedication and care. That the process yields so beautiful a flower speaks to his patience as a screenwriter. Time and again the script succeeds in cultivating an emotional seed in the viewer. That seed is nourished through human joy, pathos, sadness, empathy, awakening, and reconciliation. The resulting harvest is an emotional catharsis, one which grows organically out of his meticulous writing.

The scene which elevates the film to a higher symbolic plane begins with Officer Jim's introduction to a boy named Dixon, who calls himself 'the Prophet.' This moniker is most appropriate, for the boy weaves an ominous poetry into the film. His unique dialog foreshadows *the* awesome event which touches every character's life. As Officer Jim leaves the scene of a crime, Dixon stops him. He insists he knows the identity of the killer. To prove it he asks Jim to hear his words. Anderson slowly presses the camera toward Jim, allowing the impact of Dixon's rap to resonate: "Check that ego/come off it/I'm the prophet/the professor/I'm gonna teach you 'bout the worm/who eventually turned to catch wreck with the neck of a long-time oppressor/and he's running from the devil/but the debt is always gaining/and if he's worth being hurt/he's worth bringin' pain in/when the sunshine don't work/the good Lord bring the rain in."

Jim pays no attention to the riddle, dismissing the boy as a would-be rapper, letting the truthfulness of his message sail over his head. But Dixon is indeed a prophet, and the bizarre imagery of his rap is not far removed from biblical depictions of wheels within wheels and lakes of fire. Again, this decision of Anderson's to employ a quasi-biblical vocabulary is distinctly rooted in his sensibility. Although his art never promotes a religious agenda, Anderson comprehends the Bible and its place in Western art. He understands it intuitively and borrows from it in the construction of his cinema. This gives his work an enduring quality, yet avoids the pitfall of tethering his product to any religious organization.

The film soon pivots to another personal inferno. Stanley, the diminutive main attraction in Jimmy Gator's game-show 'What Do Kids Know,' sits alone at a library table surrounded by books espousing facts, figures, and historical accounts. His love of knowledge is surpassed only by his emotional need for paternal affection. Sadly his father only values him as a commodity; urging him on to more lucrative victories. The irony here is palpable: Stanley possesses the ability to find everything he needs in books — everything but a father's love.

The theme of fatherly dysfunction runs very strong throughout the film, corrupting the personal relationships of Frank and Earl, Claudia and Jimmy, Stanley and Rick, and even Dixon and 'the Worm.' Much of the film is a meditation on the difficulty of reconciling years of emotional (or sexual) abuse from fathers; and as usual Anderson does not shy away from displaying the deep wounds in his characters' psychology. In many ways that pain acts as a unifying force, linking every character by virtue of the shared damage they endure.

But uniquely, the film also exposes the devastating toll on the psyche of the fathers themselves. Their past sins have manifested into sorrows that weigh heavily on their souls. This is especially true for Jimmy Gator, who hits rock-bottom with such certainty that he prefers self-destruction to the slow death of cancer. Much the same can be said of Earl, whose entire dialog revolves around lamentation, remorse, and lost opportunity. His cancer is a poisonous metaphor for the emotional devastation he's inflicted, now come back to haunt his body. By the film's end, Jimmy and Earl realize a certain transformation — each in different ways. Of all the father-figures, only Rick Spector is left unchanged by the conclusion. In his character Anderson gives us a glimpse of the other two men at earlier stages of life — still callous and unappreciative of the unique bond between father and son. In turn, their weary sense of regret provides a glimpse of just how Rick is destined to end his days.

Another major theme in the film centers on unrequited love. The figure who most clearly suffers this malady is 'Quiz Kid' Donnie Smith, whose infatuation with a young bartender named Brad proves deeply humiliating. First, Brad does not return Donnie's love. He's an average bartender of below-average wit, whose only claim to fame is an attractive physique. Nevertheless, he sparks a flame of passion in Donnie which fuels all manner of misguided activity. Donnie becomes convinced he needs dental surgery — not because his teeth are deformed, but because Brad wears braces. He demands the money from his bosses, which ultimately costs him his job. Now out of work and awash in emotional confusion, he wallows in the bar where he finally confesses his love for Brad. Brad responds with muted indifference. He wants nothing to do with the once-famed Quiz-Kid.

Donnie is a desolate figure, a lonely satellite seeking a warm star to surround. He invests his emotional well-being in Brad, believing his love will be fully returned. "My name is Donnie Smith and I have lots of love to give," he sighs. But his heartfelt declaration is left to hang in midair, finding no recipient and no return. So he trades that emotional turmoil for rage and blame; willfully deciding to rob his bosses' business. To make another comparison to Hitchcock's 'Psycho,' this decision is not unlike Marion's foolish theft of the $40,000. Unfortunately, neither of these characters makes a capable thief, and by the time each of them realize their respective mistakes it's too late.

In almost all of Anderson's films, the role of divine intervention becomes crucial to the resolution between characters. Here it makes its first appearance early, inspiring the 'random' meeting between Officer Jim Kurring and Claudia Wilson. This is a special kind of chance encounter. Claudia, in the aftermath of her father's confrontation, sits alone in her apartment, drowning herself in music and cocaine. The racket creates a disturbance which Jim is dispatched to investigate. He bangs on the door, and after a noisy exchange Claudia opens it. In the blink of an eye Jim experiences a quiet rush of desire for this reticent figure. Claudia, however, is not so captivated. She sees Jim as an officer of the law intruding on her business. But she allows him in, and over time lets her guard down. She soon treats him like an invited guest. Again, the symbolism which surrounds Jim's character—a police officer who represents good; a man who kneels before the Cross—makes him a kind of blessed figure. His fateful encounter with Claudia cannot be interpreted as mere chance for the simple reason that Anderson cloaks him in the garb of moral goodness. He's a devotional figure, one who seeks (as the very same actor did in 'Hard Eight') a soul mate.

Anderson develops their relationship with a wonderful sense of artistry. In a key scene between them, he brilliantly borrows an aria from Georges Bizet's 'Carmen' to lend lyrical depth to their budding romance. In French, the line reads: "Love is a mystery you dare not refuse." Cunningly, this same line is sung by Stanley in the prior scene, providing a subtle connection between characters who will never meet.

Like Buck Swope's New Years Eve surprise in 'Boogie Nights,' Anderson grants the gift of love to Jim and Claudia. Again, Anderson sees the world as a difficult place—but never so difficult that love cannot blossom. Even the most cursory survey of his work reveals a consistent devotion to this most basic human need. Parenthetically, it's also worth noting that in all of his films Anderson introduces the male romantic character first. John in 'Hard Eight,' Buck in 'Boogie Nights,' Jim in 'Magnolia,' Barry in 'Punch Drunk Love,' H.W. in 'There Will Be Blood,' and even Freddie in 'The Master' (although his romantic portrayal is atypical). This is no accident, for the Lord introduced Adam to the world before all other creations.

Light Showers. 99% Humidity. Winds SE 12 mph

Halfway through the film, amid a torrent of cleansing rain, the cold truth begins to chill each character to the bone. Donnie realizes his love for Brad will never be requited, Phil loses faith that he'll ever reach T.J. Mackie, Linda fills a prescription of liquid morphine for Earl, Stanley wets himself in the middle of a televised broadcast, Mackie admits that his father is alive and his mother is dead, and Jimmy collapses onstage. These events signal a rupture in each character's emotional dam; the cracks have grown too large to contain the gathered pressure. The strain is made palpable by Anderson's rapt concentration behind the camera, pressing in close to the trauma experienced by each of them. The momentum now becomes deliriously accelerated. Decisions are made; free will is exercised for the first time. This is the crucial turning point in the film's progression. No longer is anyone simply pulled back and forth through space; now these characters make choices—each determined to take fate into their own hands.

Unraveling the concept of free will in Anderson's work is complicated because his artistry suggests a suspicion of human will. More often than not he prefers to move his characters into their respective situations through chance encounter tinged with an aura of divinity. Think of Dirk in 'Boogie Nights,' or John in 'Hard Eight,' or Freddie in 'The Master.' None are the architect of their own fortunes, rather each is shaped by some intervening force (Sydney for John,

Jack for Dirk, Dodd for Freddie). Indeed, in 'Magnolia' the very premise of the film (as presented in the overture) suggests a world devoid of human will, concluding: "These strange things happen all the time." This declaration implies a predetermined universe where free will plays little part in human consequence. At the same time Anderson sometimes (especially in the third act of his films) overthrows this concept, insisting his characters 'decide' upon some willful course of action. This dichotomy reveals Anderson's own struggle with the concepts of will and fate. The competition between those forces ultimately strengthens his cinematic expression.

As mentioned, Anderson tends to reserve instances of willful activity for the last act of his films. It's fair to say that only Daniel Plainview in 'There Will Be Blood' exerts a willful decisiveness right from the start. More often, as in 'Magnolia,' characters move from one experience to the next as a result of mere routine. So, Frank Mackie's schedule consists of beginning a seminar, then allowing himself to be interviewed, then concluding that seminar. And that's what he does. It's not until the film's last act that he breaks from that routine and makes the crucial decision to see his father. Similarly, Officer Jim commits no decisive act until he asks Claudia on a date; not just breaking his routine but breaking the rules of police conduct. Donnie's first decisive action (beyond declaring his love for Brad) is to rob his bosses' warehouse. Stanley too follows routine until he decides not to participate in the game show's final round, actively wetting his pants in the process. And at the end of the film, Jimmy decides to take his own life; as does Linda. Only divine intervention prevents the success of either.

Of all Anderson's characters only Phil, the guardian angel of the film, makes a willful decision early in the narrative: to find Frank Mackie. It's a conscious act which defines the selflessness of his character, and eventually brings him spiritual reward. In the case of the other players (Jim and Claudia excluded), the outcome of their decisions are not so valedictory. Because Anderson's world is conceived of flawed gods and lost men, bad decisions are the rule rather than the exception—which in turn reflects the fallen states of his characters. Rarely does he allow them happiness when they rely on their own decisiveness; rather they must defer to a guiding force for the salvation they cannot attain on their own.

Jimmy Gator exemplifies this motif. Near the end of the film he finally decides to take his own life—only to be saved by one of the most miraculous events in any of Anderson's movies: a frog crashes through the skylight of his home, striking the pistol from his hand just as the shot is fired. Jimmy is literally saved by a force from heaven; a rain of frogs transposed from the biblical book of Exodus. On a deeper level, this moment depicts an artistic battleground for Anderson. Divine intervention vs. willful human action. In this round (as in most), heavenly intervention is the victor.

*

As the storm gathers force, the film accelerates toward resolution. The personal drama intensifies. Heated emotional turbulence forms the heartbeat of the film, and here the narrative reaches critical mass. Jimmy's game-show nearly falls apart as both he and Stanley experience a different kind of internal stress. Stanley only wants to go to the bathroom but soon realizes the staff doesn't care. From their perspective, his only purpose is to answer the questions put before him. Worse, his Dad doesn't care either. To him Stanley is little more than a thoroughbred racer — and God help him if his legs give out. At the same time, Jimmy's race is run. He's at the end of his days and harbors no illusions of personal solace. He comes unhinged, inadvertently giving away the answers to the quiz in a fog of delirium: "It's Chopin. Very recognizable piece, uh, Marche Militaire. That's the answer. I wasn't supposed to give. . . but it's Chopin. . . Sing us a ditty, guys. A Chopin ditty. . ." His physical collapse sets off a frenzy of activity during which it's learned that Stanley wet his pants. His father confronts him without even trying to temper his disgust: "What the fuck did you do that for!?" It's a line Jimmy himself might have inflicted on Claudia — or Earl on Frank — many years before. Throughout the film these echoes of paternal cruelty resonate through the characters' shared psychology. Connections are then made in the viewer's mind, revealing father-figures who wear the same mask at different stages of life: Rick, a younger version of Jimmy; Jimmy, a younger version of Earl.

Meanwhile, Guinevere, the journalist questioning Frank Mackie, has cracked the veneer of his careful exterior to reveal the troubled psyche beneath. She confirms that his father is alive and his mother is dead. In fact, Earl abandoned his family when Frank was just a boy, leaving him alone to care for his ailing mother. Forced to watch her die of cancer, the seeds of Frank's 'Seduce and Destroy' seminar were sewn.

Her death was interpreted as an abandonment—just as Earl had abandoned him earlier. Now Frank was totally alone. From that point on his pain would be transformed into something obscene and invincible through which he could conquer human emotions. No longer would he be hurt by love or crippled by dependence. He made sure his new persona could tower over every feeling—then unleashed this same persona on all women, symbolically directing his childish scorn back upon his parental demons. The sad irony here (and a perceptive social commentary) is that his demented quest to manipulate women was rewarded with celebrity, fame, and fortune.

Anderson scours a well of despair as the film spirals downward, exposing raw wounds while demanding his characters face their tormenters. Stanley must endure his father's disgust and disdain. Linda must face the inevitable fact that she'll soon be alone. Jimmy must bear the burden of paternal failure in a cancerous body. And Frank must face the woman who exposes his lies. Again, it is raw truth which hits these characters hardest and becomes their most tenacious persecutor. Every character must come to terms with the awful truths of their past and present lives. This dominant theme is summed up perfectly by Jimmy Gator: "The Book says we might be through with the past, but the past ain't through with us." This is the film's mantra—and a mantra for nearly all of Anderson's cinema.

The camera moves over a plane of emotional upheaval, cleaving through broken dreams and sad regrets, revealing the depths of common trauma. Yet from this wasteland, as so often happens in Anderson's tragedies, a small gesture of hope emerges. Jim asks Claudia on a date, and she says 'yes.'

That act, between two figures who channel Anderson's expression of redemptive love, again delivers the film from any sense of total hopelessness. Just when the circumstances of his narrative seem the bleakest, Anderson sparks a gesture of goodwill to illuminate his subtle faith in humanity.

At this point he allows his characters a chance to reflect. This is important, because it signals Anderson's overall sympathy for their plight. He's not an overlord; he does not inflict wrath upon his characters for no reason. Rather, he sets them on difficult journeys which proceed from suffering to solace. He respects them enough to allow moments of self-awareness to inform their actions. For example, Stanley makes the decision not to play the bonus-round, asserting: "I don't want to do it anymore. I'm not a doll to entertain you." Donnie too finally accepts the unrequited nature of his love for Brad. "It's a dangerous thing to confuse children with angels!" scolds Thurston from the end of the bar, giving voice to Anderson's biblical vocabulary. Frank Mackie too is given a chance to reflect, pausing to consider whether he should accept the fateful phone call from his dying father (via Phil).

One of the most devastating instances of self-awareness and reflection—even confession—occurs in a dialog between Jimmy and his wife, Rose, late in the film. He divulges, slowly, clumsily, that he may have sexually abused his daughter when she was a child. His wife's response is culled from an awful harvest of emotions; her painful wail the torment of a Greek tragedy. It's a hellish scene, filled with accumulated pathos and despair for the irreversible harm inflicted on Claudia, and the exposed lies that ruin a family.

Many miles away, Linda's moment of reflection results in a decision not to administer a dose of liquid morphine to Earl. She cannot bring herself to void his mental life; cannot bear witness to his languorous death. Because she dare not face the world alone she decides to end her own life instead. This act of abandonment coupled with her decision not to administer the morphine fully captures the duality of her character. On the one hand she assigns no value to her own life; on the other she assigns a value to his — despite the fact that he's already dying. Ironically it's only through this near-fatal decision that her love for Earl finally, truthfully, emerges; at last untainted by selfish motive.

It is then left to Phil, the merciful angel of death, to administer the final dose of morphine. This somber sequence represents Anderson's cautious ode to assisted suicide, allowing death to bring a quiet end to human suffering. When Earl finally passes away later in the film, having beheld his estranged son, his death will foster a sense of rebirth. This measured sequence represents an artistic declaration on Anderson's part, drawing a powerful contrast to the film's opening overture. In that segment, life and death are made pointless through coincidental tragedy. Here, Earl's death is made meaningful, even poignant, through the final words he bequeaths to his son.

The entire sequence unfolds as a shared experience of love and mercy; from the empathy in Phil's expression as he administers the morphine to the pure catharsis experienced by Frank when his father speaks to him for the last time. In this, the most intimate passage of the film, Anderson articulates a mature pronouncement of divinity's role in transforming that which might sometimes seem pointless —

life and death—into a scene of affirmation and redemptive beauty.

For Jim and Claudia, reflection comes through their awakening love for one another. Their date begins unassumingly, but soon the intimacy of the moment unearths a buried anxiety in each, particularly Claudia. She begins to come apart, spilling out a cacophony of self-loathing and apology: "I'm really nervous that you're gonna hate me soon. You're gonna find stuff out about me and you're gonna hate me," all of which catches Jim off-guard. Yet in his reply he summons the courage to meet her gesture with equal vulnerability, confessing: "I lost my gun today. And I'm the laughing stock of a lot of people. . . You said we should tell each other things. Well, I can tell you this: I feel like a fool. And I'm scared that once you find that out, you might not like me." The words flow like water through the desert of Claudia's soul.

Their dialog signifies a rare honesty between characters in the film, very different from the lies which cripple almost every other relationship. Anderson rewards these two with a hopeful gesture: Claudia asks Jim if he wants to kiss her, he says yes, and as they lean across the table Anderson presses the camera very close. The shot blossoms like a cinematic exclamation point, brightening the sense of joyful discovery between them. Unfortunately the moment proves fleeting, as the emotional weight of their union (and its implications) prove too much for Claudia to bear. She flees the restaurant, taking refuge in the familiar confines of her lonely apartment.

By this point Anderson has whipped up a terrific intensity, creating a sense of immediate personal urgency.

Frank Mackie finally enters Earl's home, coming face to face with his father. He sits beside him and unleashes a wrathful tirade, castigating Earl for his past abandonment, leveling him with foul language and imperial judgment even as he breaks down in tears. "I hate your fucking guts! I hope you die. Goddamm you fucking asshole—you fucking asshole—I hate you! You fucking. . . you fu. . . don't leave." These last heartbreaking words reawaken the abandoned child buried deep in Mackie's psyche. So naked, so brutal, is the image that even Phil must avert his eyes from the searing pain. Earl lays dormant, unresponsive to either his son or the world around him.

Rain Clearing. Breezy Overnight

The inner-trauma of these figures inevitably metastasizes into a storm of unearthly magnitude. Every character in the film will be touched by Anderson's most ambitious artistic gesture thus far: a monumental rain of frogs. The groundwork for this shared moment of truth is laid in a heady sequence. In an effort to unify all of his characters, Anderson inserts Aimee Mann's lyrics into each of their mouths; allowing each of them to say the same thing, to express the same despair: "It's not going to stop, until you wise up. No, it's not going to stop. . . so just give up." This linked scene provides a surreal example of Anderson's intuitive grasp of the boundary between cinema and theater;

here crafting a shared lament that sets the stage for a more harrowing catharsis.

As Linda is raced to the hospital after another suicide attempt; as Stanley sits alone in the library; as Officer Jim spies Donnie attempting to return stolen loot; as Rose Gator arrives outside Claudia's apartment; as Claudia sits alone in the dark; as Frank weeps at the bedside of his dying father; and as Jimmy prepares to blow his own brains out, it *happens*. An impossible rain of frogs falls freely from the sky like tears from a flawed god. It's a supernatural maelstrom that incarnates Dixon's earlier prophecy: "When the sun don't shine, the good Lord bring the rain in." And indeed for every character's vast emotional void, this rain is manna from Heaven. It gives definite shape and texture to their individual moments of truth—as Claudia embraces her mother, as Stanley sees a world outside his books, as Donnie recedes into Officer Jim's arms, and as Jimmy Gator's gun is deflected by a careening frog.

Jimmy's salvation is most symbolic, for it allows the possibility of a resolution between himself and his abused daughter. In this rain his life is spared for a greater purpose. He's accorded something very rare in life: a second chance. Again, this act of divine providence exemplifies Anderson's faith in human redemption. It doesn't matter that the resolution between Jimmy and Claudia does not occur in the context of the film; it matters only that the possibility lives.

Nowhere is the personal resolution more gracefully articulated than in the closing scene between Frank Mackie and his father. Earl, awakened by the clamor of crashing frogs, near death, slowly turns to his estranged son. In a moment of breathless recognition, he struggles to utter the words he so desperately wants to say: "I love you." Frank looks on, spellbound with childlike wonder at the massive effort his father puts into these dying words. Anderson's artistry is too subtle to let him complete the phrase, emphasizing instead the nobility and perseverance of the gesture itself, so very like the sublime magnolia. Earl's effort to bridge the chasm that separates him from his son forms the emotional denouement of the film. It's the moment where the narrative's collected sense of anguish is distilled into one enduring gesture of love, made all the more ironic by virtue of its deadly context. Like the mythical Phoenix, a new sense of life is born from this closure; allowing resurrection from death, granting Frank the possibility of emotional repair. Again this sequence represents a total repudiation of the meaningless death in the film's overture.

This climax, to include the rain of frogs itself, could only come from a mature artist fully confident of his ability. It exemplifies Anderson's daring as a filmmaker, revealing an auteur who would rather take a chance and fall short than play it safe and remain stagnant. Here he does not disappoint, finding within himself a vision so abstract, so complete, that it may someday represent the most purely artistic moment in any of his films. More pertinently, only a gesture this big, this omnipotent, could possibly conclude the enormous symphony of activity witnessed to this point in the film. Any smaller movement would have only diminished the finale's impact.

Anderson's investment in this symbolic rain marks an effort to define a truism in his art; namely that coincidence exists in the universe to be sure—but that concepts like hope and love do not emerge from random, meaningless, acts of chance. Rather, sheer coincidence is a subordinate mechanism to a more divine guidance. That guidance makes itself known to one and all (given the right circumstance), and shepherds them into personal affirmation. His world of flawed gods and lost men descends from biblical parable and even Greek tragedy; describing human movement through activity that is propelled by external force. 'Magnolia' begins with a clever depiction of fate, drawn in the overture to the film. But over time he shapes instances of serendipity into more unifying, more purposeful, and more life-affirming relationships. By the end of the film, Anderson's great rain acts as an awakening force; one that enlightens every character. Each of them become aware of personal truths and the emotional solace that emerges from their acceptance. The great rain does not wash away their sins, it underscores the importance of owning them. This in turn brings each character a step closer to redemption. A change in emotional attitude is harvested from this rain, opening new avenues of healing through shared moments of realization. Each of these characters now possess the power to imagine what is possible.

So Now Then.

Anderson provides a rewarding epilogue in the film's closing scenes, moving from one character to another, depicting the emotional harbor each of them has reached. Stanley vocalizes his desire for simple respect, proclaiming:

"You have to be nice to me." His father only sends him to bed; but within this declaration the seeds of resolution are sewn. Meanwhile, Donnie returns the money he stole from his boss. That act, together with his conversation with Jim, suggest a new awakening for him as well. As Jim reminds us: "Sometimes people need to be forgiven." Elsewhere, Frank emerges from Earl's home more emotionally complete than prior to his meeting. The act of witnessing his father die, and hearing his last words, delivers him into a greater emotional stability. Jimmy Gator remains alive, saved from suicide, now prepared to repair the emotional rift between himself and his daughter. Much the same can be said for Linda, who lives to see a new day. Alone now, her emotional gulf is uniquely self-contained, and must be bridged internally.

Lastly, there is the quiet reunion of Jim and Claudia. Anderson constructs this scene with poetic subtlety, never allowing visual flair to detract from purity of emotion. It's a study in minimalism as Jim cautiously enters her room and sits beside her. Rather than exposing Jim's face, Anderson trains the camera on Claudia, following the evolution of her expression as Jim speaks to her. Aimee Mann's 'Save Me' plays over the scene, suggesting an unspoken salvation for Claudia manifested in the good figure of Jim. His last words to her are poignant and truthful: "If you want to be with me, then be with me," fully respecting her worth as a person. The camera frames her face, resting the full emotional weight of the film on her natural reaction. And slowly, surely, without artifice or false-light, she smiles.

'The Book says we might be through with the past, but the past ain't through with us.' That phrase, uttered at key moments in the film, sums up the trial each of these figures has endured. In the end, their collective journey has delivered them to a place where genuine healing — however small — can begin. Nowhere is this better conveyed than in the quiet smile that crosses Claudia's face as the film comes to an end. It's the image which most succinctly captures the glimmer of hope at the bottom of Pandora's box.

'Magnolia' remains perhaps the most complex and ambitious of all Anderson's films, particularly in representing visual symbol. Like 'Hard Eight' and 'Boogie Nights' before it, Anderson confirms the central place that divine intervention occupies in his art. In fashioning an architecture to communicate this principal, Anderson begins the film on a theme of random coincidence. But because random chance is devoid of meaning, he replaces it over time with a more sophisticated, more meaningful doctrine. Divine guidance and human goodwill; these are the harbingers of hope and love, both rooted in design.

This doctrine is crucial to interpreting the mysterious rain of frogs which represents, to this point, the summit of Anderson's art. In the book of Exodus, Chapter 8, Moses speaks: "Let my people go, and if thou refuse to let them go, behold, I will smite all thy borders with frogs." In 'Magnolia,' Anderson's omnipotent rain waters his characters like flowers, allowing them to open up. This emotional release removes them from the bondage of personal regret and failure. In this context, Earl's death embodies the purest expression of release. It is the sole sacrifice the film demands for the community's sense of shared resurrection.

This monumental work of Anderson's, replete with dense religious symbolism, marks the highpoint of his allegiance to divine modes of representation. His next film,

'Punch Drunk Love' signals an astute turning point in his growth as an artist; a chamber-piece which returns Anderson to new artistic beginnings.

Part Four:

PUNCH DRUNK LOVE

*

By the time 'Punch Drunk Love' received its debut, P.T. Anderson had been a serious filmmaker for ten years. Over the course of a decade he had honed a precise visual style, demonstrated a natural affinity for ensemble narrative, and mastered a divine mode of representation. Were he so inclined, 'Punch Drunk Love' too could have been a large-scale effort replete with flawed gods and lost men. Instead Anderson chose to reflect upon his own body of work, and reinvent himself.

A careful viewing of 'Punch Drunk Love' reveals a dynamic shift in his thematic vocabulary, and a more focused attention to individual motive. The film feels pared-down, revealing an economy not seen since 'Hard Eight.' Perhaps the sheer breadth and spectacle of 'Magnolia' fomented a yearning for artistic minimalism. Perhaps he simply didn't want to be pigeonholed as a particular kind of filmmaker. Whatever the reason, through this film Anderson seems determined to renew his artistry. Emerging in the aftermath of 'Boogie Nights' and 'Magnolia,' the piece feels almost completely detached from his previous body of cinema. The result is a fresh, luminous work which remains true to Anderson's aesthetic foundation. It also signals a turning point. Like a Janus-face, the film looks backward to narrative elements found in his early art, but also forward to new modes of individual declaration through character. The visual symbolism strikes a new chord; one that proves so successful that it will resonate profoundly through his next effort, 'There Will Be Blood.'

The narrative opens simply on the image of a man sitting at a desk. But for the bright blue suit he wears, the shot is devoid of color. Anderson composes the picture by setting the man, Barry Egan, deep against the corner, occupying a minimal area of visual space. We sense this figure himself is 'cornered,' perhaps by the people around him, perhaps by circumstance. The shot establishes a focused economy, surrounding the isolated subject with nothing of visual interest. The eye is drawn solely to the blue man, set in relief. This further creates a sense of scale. Barry Egan is a small man; a lonely man. His problems are comprised of the minutia, the tediousness, of life. Anderson's design here is not pejorative. Quite the contrary, his preference has always been to fashion drama from the day-to-day plight of the Everyman. Barry's small problems and peculiarities are the substance of the film. By the end of his unique journey, Barry Egan will become one of Anderson's most secure, well-rewarded characters.

We quickly grasp that Barry's life is unremarkable. He enjoys his job to a certain extent, and his appearance reflects a modest pride. His interpersonal skills are somewhat awkward, but not incompetent. Beyond these surface characteristics, Barry is a man who does not exert control over his own life. Rather his behavior is more often manipulated by others. Specifically, seven overbearing sisters who make a plaything of his emotional stability. Over the years this tyranny has created insecurity and anxiety for Barry. His physical movements at this point in the film, particularly around his sisters, reveal an emotional reticence coupled with an inability to communicate his frustration. Barry is a sympathetic figure; exactly the type of misfit for whom Anderson typically conjures good fortune. The uniqueness of 'Punch Drunk Love' comes in the manner by which Barry is delivered into that good fortune.

Barry sits at his desk, conversing on the phone with a 'Healthy Choice' representative about a peculiar promotional campaign. The discovery he makes concerning their coupons will play a role in his future actions (indeed, the entire film is a series of discoveries), but for now the discussion comes to an end. He leaves his desk, and walks outside. There he witnesses something altogether unusual: a moving vehicle overturns and crashes. The impact is ferocious, and Barry is taken aback. At that exact moment, a van pulls up to the curb near Barry and deposits a strange object on the sidewalk. The van disappears; all is silent. The object resembles a miniature piano. Barry, bewildered by this bizarre sequence of events, retreats into his office.

From this inexplicable incident, over the course of the film, Barry reinvents himself completely. The strange allure of the harmonium (the small piano), and its symbolic appearance from nowhere, is a declarative gesture on Anderson's part. On one level it hearkens back to the symbolism of previous films, where some saving grace is unexpectedly delivered to an important character. But on another level, Anderson's harmonium is conceived as something new, abstract, and decidedly human.

To this point his symbols have been generally tethered to biblical reference-points. In 'Magnolia,' the rain of frogs has its roots in the book of Exodus. In 'Boogie Nights,' the cash received by Buck occurs in the context of Christmas. But in 'Punch Drunk Love,' the harmonium has no tie to any biblical point of origin. Nor does the setting, time, or motive derive from any religious association or intimation. To produce music the instrument must be played by human hands, suggesting the control Barry must summon to make it sound. It's an empowering device; one Barry must willfully master if any harmony is to come from it. This self-generated harmony foreshadows the active path he must travel to secure a lasting happiness; all of it very humanly derived. It's as if, in seeking a new language of visual symbol for the film, Anderson sought to divorce himself from exclusively divine imagery.

Again, the harmonium represents, most literally, harmony. It is the harmony so clearly missing from Barry's life. More specifically, it anticipates the emotional harmony soon to materialize in the form of Lena Leonard, who delivers her car for repair at the garage adjacent to Barry's business. Like the harmonium, her appearance in Barry's life is spontaneous. She seems to come from nowhere, placed in front of Barry solely for his discovery. Later it's revealed she works with one of his sisters, and inquired about him after seeing his picture. Lena's romantic motives seem derived from the phrase: 'opposites attract.' At one point in the film she tells Barry that she has no siblings at all, unlike his seven sisters. "I'm the exact opposite," she smiles. Here it's fair to say that Lena is fascinated by Barry, the lone male surrounded by a flock of women. Her desire for him is largely rooted in the uniqueness of his person. For Lena, opposites not only attract—they create harmony. Indeed, she's best understood as a living instrument of harmony; one Barry must actively, carefully, learn to play.

This level of artistic sophistication is remarkable, especially when understood in the context of Anderson's prior cinema. 'Cigarettes and Coffee' began Anderson's quest to infuse his imagery with precise symbolism. The ominous twenty-dollar bill that touches the lives of each character manifests the tragic adage: 'money is the root of all evil.' In 'Hard Eight,' the closing shot, so carefully crafted around the red blemish on Sydney's cuff, exemplifies the dark presence of spilled blood. His next film displays even greater ambition, both in the cleansing pools which symbolize Dirk's baptism, and in Buck's heavenly Christmas gift. In 'Magnolia' his ambition reaches an apex, overwhelming the theater with spiritual rain. In 'Punch Drunk Love' however, the core of his symbolism is stripped of its biblical garb. The film is further stripped of peripheral character. Unlike his two previous films, so highly populated, here there are only three characters of substance: Barry, Lena, and the harmonium. The remaining cast function as orbiting vessels who challenge Barry's emerging desire to master his own fate.

Barry retrieves the small piano from the street. Later, Lena correctly identifies it as a harmonium. This is appropriate given her symbolic link to the instrument—in many ways its living incarnation. Barry secures it in his office, away from prying eyes, and begins to appreciate the bizarre sounds it utters. His interaction with the instrument is soothing, even reciprocal. It creates within him an unprecedented sense of peace. Every time he touches the instrument he's provided both awareness and motivation. His relationship to it (or more accurately, with it) becomes unique, and the scenes which feature its absence prove turbulent.

Barry is a figure for whom the world is an unstable place devoid of emotional balance. The harmonium — and by extension Lena — will provide that balance for him if he can master the opportunity they represent. In the meantime he continues going about his business, selling mail-order 'funjers' (novelty plungers) to various institutions; even as he fends off the hectic demands of his seven sisters. It's fitting that his stock and trade is the sale of plungers, since so much of his life (figuratively) is in the toilet.

*

At about this point in the film, Anderson fills the entire screen with a field of abstract shape and color. These plastic interludes (designed by artist Jeremy Blake) can be interpreted many ways. First, they suggest the emotional turbulence of the film's characters at key moments. They also function as surreal gateways; sometimes foreshadowing future scenes, sometimes using sounds to imply conflict or desire. But ultimately these mesmerizing color-schemes reveal Anderson's understanding of this most visual medium; exemplifying the maxim that images alone speak a thousand words. They trigger abstract thought-processes that take the viewer through internal modes of conceptualizing emotion and circumstance.

Anderson's use of color is striking not just in these sequences, but in the representation of Barry and Lena themselves. First, he's always dressed in blue. This might seem a mere reflection of his melancholy demeanor, but when combined with the flood of white light unleashed throughout the film, and Lena's ubiquitous red dress, the visual palette becomes a rich canvas of red, white, and blue. It's a bold visual gesture that matches the minimalism of the film's architecture which keeps itself contained to three central characters; so very different from his two previous films. This red white and blue color-scheme signifies certain implications for his principal characters, particularly Barry.

Meanwhile, Barry's sister Elizabeth bullies him into attending a party she's hosting. She wants to introduce Barry to an unnamed 'friend,' but he'll have no part of it. He feels intuitively set up, pressed into yet another corner. Despite his reservations he finally shows up. Here Anderson offers an unenviable glimpse of Barry's submissive relationship to his sisters. As he walks through the door he can hear them ridiculing him; but instead of leaving altogether or putting a stop to their bullying, he simply walks into the maelstrom. This acceptance of abuse implies a damaged psychology, made numb over the years by repeated harassment. Barry absorbs their disparaging remarks in a good-natured way, but this must be considered a façade. Under the surface, he's emotionally wounded. He doesn't want to be here, nor does he fit in. Over the course of the film his frustrations manifest themselves in uncontainable fits of rage—until the moment he takes it upon himself to put a stop to his sisters' abuse.

His emotional demons emerge for the first time at Elizabeth's party, where he takes a hammer and shatters a glass partition in her house. Later, in confidence, Barry confesses to her husband: "I don't like myself. . . sometimes I cry for no reason. Can you help me?" It's a vulnerable scene, given a comic punch-line when Elizabeth's husband reminds him: "Barry, I'm a dentist." Yet it's in this scene that a real empathy for Barry's character is established. Feelings of insecurity and loneliness — of not being able to fit in anywhere — are commonplace in a world so diverse and hierarchical as our own. Like many of Anderson's most important characters, Barry is a small 'e' everyman searching for solace without quite knowing where to find it.

He returns to his lonely apartment which, like his office, seems entirely devoid of color. The drab earth-tones that dominate the room all but swallow up Barry's blue suit. Here again the composition implies a solitary existence. The furnishings are bare, and the décor gives no clue to his personal interests. His home seems little more than the space he occupies when he's not at work. He sits at the kitchen table, clipping Healthy Choice coupons, when he happens to notice an advertisement for a sex-chat line. 'Lonely?' the ad wonders; and indeed Barry is lonely.

This scene provides a comic glimpse into Barry's mental peculiarities. His interest in 'Healthy Choice' coupons stems from a promotional campaign which allows the labels of their products to be exchanged for frequent flier miles. That interest becomes a full-blown obsession when he realizes that the miles awarded for some products far exceed the cost of the product itself. This strikes Barry as a potential treasure trove — which he intends to mine. The fact that he doesn't want to travel anywhere seems beside the point; nor does it seem pertinent that he's never flown on a plane. His mind has latched on to this opportunity and refuses to let go. As he reminds a co-worker: "Frequent flier miles are like currency these days."

This scene also depicts Barry's physical peculiarities, which emerge from a simple desire to connect with someone of the opposite sex. He inevitably calls the sex chat-line for no other reason than to assuage his own loneliness. Because he lacks the wherewithal to make a real romantic connection, he's literally reduced to paying for it. Later in the film, he figuratively 'pays' as well, in the form of harassment by the chat-line personnel. For now, this scene fashions a thematic dichotomy in which Barry is revealed to be a little askew in his various pursuits, both mentally and physically. The Healthy Choice scheme eventually falls apart (just when he needs it most) and his call to the chat-line yields similarly negative consequences.

In truth, Barry will not be made whole — either in mind or body — through these peripheral pursuits. They are distractions more than anything else, which prevent him from attaining true personal fulfillment. In many ways he's reminiscent of Buck Swope in 'Boogie Nights,' who made every effort to find the right 'fit' through a variety of misguided fashion choices. It wasn't until he realized a genuine love for Jessie that he began to be personally validated and rewarded. Here, Barry's actions are just as clumsy, and his decisions just as wrong-headed. He has not yet found the right 'fit,' and like Buck he's doomed to be the butt of every joke until he discovers something real and meaningful. Unlike Buck, Barry's love will not emerge under passive circumstances. He must find the will to secure it through active pursuit. Again this illustrates Anderson's faith in the redemptive power of love; so often the saving grace for his most dysfunctional characters.

As established in previous chapters, Anderson does not allow his characters the convenience of instant gratification. Instead he mandates a more difficult odyssey to attain personal solace. He makes demands of his characters. They never arrive at their destination without suffering, nor are they rewarded for taking the easiest route. Barry will not overcome his loneliness through a sex chat-line, rather his reward will come from a real love that must be physically fought for. As he declares to the Mattress Man near the end of the film: "I have a love in my life that makes me stronger than anything you can imagine."

By the same token, Barry will not attain mental 'wholeness' by amassing coupons for bonus miles he'll never use. Rather his mind must work its way through the emotional dilemmas in his life; particularly those surrounding his sibling relationships. To this effort Anderson grants him the harmonium; a lodestone through which he's transformed from a man whose free will is usurped by his sisters, to a man whose will is strengthened through the power of love. Only then does he discover the courage to confront his emotional demons, and attain a meaningful peace. In this long arc, Anderson distills the entire film into one character's inner-development. Barry evolves from a man of misplaced direction to a man of purpose and will; all of it inspired by the discovery of harmony through love.

In constructing the narrative, Anderson builds upon past examples of romance. John and Clementine in 'Hard Eight,' Jim and Claudia in 'Magnolia;' and above all Buck and Jessie in 'Boogie Nights.' These romantic ancestors provide the template for Barry and Lena; yet here the scale is much larger given Barry's role as the principal character. Anderson no longer resigns the romantic interest of the film to the periphery. In fact, of all Anderson's films, 'Punch Drunk Love' is the one undeniable love story. His decision to apply this theme to the subtle redefinition of his own artistry shows him to be a filmmaker dedicated to the most basic human values.

*

At about the mid-point of the film, as so often happens in Anderson's narratives, things go very wrong for Barry. From Provo, Utah, home of the Mattress Man and his cohorts, a team of four brothers is dispatched to teach Barry a lesson. They intend to make him pay for what he's done. The fact that Barry hasn't done anything wrong is irrelevant. They're simply serving Anderson's theater which demands that Barry suffer for his misguided efforts. On a more subtle level, these henchmen represent a 'threat' to Barry's independence. Their function in the film is to embody the universal forces that keep him cornered and diminished; reminding us that Barry's struggle will not be fair or easy.

At the same time (again establishing a dichotomy) his first date with Lena has gone quite well. Even though the two of them are evicted from a restaurant after Barry destroys the bathroom in a fit of rage, their romantic connection proves too genuine to be ruined by peripheral concerns. They spend some time together in Lena's apartment, and Barry leaves with a handshake. "And, bye bye" is the only phrase he can summon. He chides himself as he leaves the building, then something odd occurs. In a surprising effort to reach him, Lena calls him at the front desk. Elated, he returns to her and they share their first real kiss. In that moment, Barry is given new life and new purpose. The effort Lena makes to call him back proves that his love is requited. She takes the extra step to make sure he knows their love is mutual. Again, this small scene beautifully conveys a sense of sudden discovery for Barry; one that incarnates the earlier harmony he found through the little harmonium.

But with that melody comes misfortune. Barry is aggressively taken captive by the Mattress Man's henchmen, and soon he's forced to withdraw cash from an ATM machine. They take his money, rough him up, and send him running for his life. These scenes display Anderson's ecstasy behind the camera, pressing Barry through a maze of shadow and light; a manic tour through the back-alleys and dead ends of, essentially, Barry's subconscious. The imagery is dark and striking, reminiscent of the slippery chase scenes found in the best Film Noir. Here, the chase is an active metaphor for the running Barry's done all his life. It's only when one of the brothers shouts: "Where the fuck are you goin'? We KNOW where you live!" that he finally comes to a stop, realizing that a man can't run from himself.

This event sparks an odd burst of activity on Barry's part. He arrives for work the next morning, packed with nervous energy, and hijacks Lance for a morning run to the supermarket. He must acquire more pudding. His obsessive quest to capitalize on the promotional error which allows him a wealth of frequent-flier miles proves itself the vehicle of his escape — not just from the four brothers, but into the arms of the woman he loves. This sequence is important because Barry makes a willful decision here. He must see Lena in Hawaii. Before anyone can stop him, he and Lance are gathering up as much pudding as the two of them can carry. So happy is Barry that he begins a wonderfully improvised dance in the middle of the grocery store. In many scenes like this one — and indeed throughout the film — Adam Sandler proves an inspired choice to play the part of Barry Egan. He possesses just the right combination of introverted shyness and raw physical energy to lend sympathy and unpredictability to this complex character.

Back in the office an unexpected problem arises. Barry is told by a Healthy Choice representative that, in fact, it will take several weeks to redeem his coupons for frequent-flier miles. This infuriates Barry, since his desire to be with Lena in Hawaii is immediate. Unfortunately, the realities of life have trumped the scenario in his mind. His careful plan, so precisely conceived, is now null and void due to miscalculation. The result is a terrific burst of rage. He slams his fist into the wall, revealing a series of cuts along his knuckles which spell the word 'LOVE.' It's a strange image that suggests a universal truth: love is sometimes painful. In this shot too, Barry caresses the harmonium — that symbol of inspiration — which in turn allows him to collect his wits. He makes an irreversible decision. No matter the cost, he will reach Lena in Hawaii. He ignores the coupons altogether, relying instead on his own fortitude.

The importance of this decision cannot be overemphasized because it exemplifies Barry's emerging sense of free will. If this were a film made when Anderson was younger, Barry's trip to Hawaii might have occurred via some fateful allowance. For example, coupons exchanged for frequent flier miles. But here Anderson purposely pulls the rug out from under himself. First he sets up a framework of fate/chance through this unusual device of amassing coupons, then slams the door in Barry's face by refusing him the opportunity to redeem them. This reversal of fortune signals Anderson's evolving sensibility, here deconstructing his own artistic devices. Instead of allowing fateful guidance to bring Barry and Lena together, he forces Barry to make the decision himself — despite the fact that he's afraid to fly. This decisiveness represents a repudiation of divinity's role in determining Barry's success. No longer will Anderson grant his protagonist a meaningful reward through some coincidental encounter. Rather, he insists that Barry rely on nothing more than his own will to attain personal solace. This is Barry's big discovery: that his ability to succeed lies entirely within himself. Indeed, from this moment on Barry becomes an instrument of will; determining his own actions, amassing confidence, and repairing the trauma in his life. It's also worth noting that his embrace of free will is foreshadowed in the actions of Lena much earlier. She herself is a willful actor, making the decision to ask him on a date without any external motivation; pursuing Barry solely because she desires to meet him. This too is a sign of Anderson's emerging preference for will over fate.

The playful tone of Shelly Duvall's 'He Needs Me,' frames an elegant sequence which take Barry from the troubles of his daily life to the carefree shores of Hawaii. Barry moves through a luminous corridor to board the plane almost as if transcending Earth itself. And once in Hawaii, his eagerness to see Lena manifests itself in a moment of declarative (albeit comic) assertion. He doesn't have Lena's phone number, so he calls the one person who does: his sister Elizabeth. Right on cue, she begins chiding him about where he is, and what he's doing. And Barry, in a burst of articulate rage, tells her: "You're killing me! Give me the fucking number you understand!? I'll kill you!" Of course, she gives him the number. This episode above all confirms the appearance of an entirely new Barry Egan — and by extension, a new P.T. Anderson. He, Anderson, unveils a distinct character in Barry; one who takes control of his will and exercises it to attain both supreme catharsis (with his sister) and emotional wholeness (with Lena). Artistically speaking, the creation of Barry Egan is P.T. Anderson's declaration of independence — which emerges beautifully from the red, white, and blue color-scheme of the film.

The relationship between Barry and Lena represents a great leap forward for Anderson; one which lands him quite a distance from previous films. Consider the chance encounters that brought together John and Clementine in 'Hard Eight,' Buck and Jessie in 'Boogie Nights,' and Jim and Claudia in 'Magnolia.' Those journeys of love began through fateful encounters that had little (or nothing) to do with acts of will. They found each other by chance, or through the intervention of some external force. True, Officer Jim makes a conscious effort to seek out Claudia at the end of 'Magnolia,' but it's nothing compared to the multiple challenges Barry overcomes to be with Lena.

When he finally reaches her, Anderson frames the two of them in a shot that must rank among his most endearing: Barry and Lena set in silhouette against a parade of people moving back and forth around them — a cinematic walk of life. This captivating image sets the stage for their time together in Hawaii. A lush seashore frames their dialog as gentle music mingles with the evening. Soon they're lying in bed together, and here Anderson conjures an absolutely unique instance of pillow-talk. Barry begins: "I'm looking at your face and I want to smash it with a sledge-hammer it's so pretty." And Lena replies: "I want to chew your face and scoop out your eyes and eat them." Barry smiles quietly: "This is nice." Much more than nice, these scenes represent a profound personal reward for Barry. His act of will has earned him an unprecedented harmony. The next morning he confesses to Lena: "I didn't come here for business, I came here for you."

So new to Barry are these experiences, and so securely do they center his emotional bearing, that in short order he makes an entire series of decisions. He begins with a phone call to the chat-line causing him so much trouble. He demands they return his money or the police will be contacted. And this is only the beginning. Barry doesn't confine his new sense of self-worth to Hawaii; instead he nurtures his emotional liberation with active resolve, strengthened by his fully requited love for Lena. Like many of Anderson's most important characters, he seems a phoenix risen from the ashes.

When Barry and Lena return home, he's tested by physical peril. But this is a different Barry; one who's finally learned to love himself. The profound devotion he feels for Lena, returned in full, has not only granted him new purpose, but new validation as well. He no longer feels alone in the world; rather he's become part of something greater than himself—a more perfect union. If this union possesses value, then he must possess value as well. It's a feeling which broadens Barry's understanding of himself and the world. It connects him in a way that dissolves his sense of alienation. Barry has finally discovered that he belongs.

It is in this context that he's mortally challenged, again by the four brothers from Utah. They smash into his car as he and Lena return from the airport, sending the vehicle spinning into the night. When it stops, Barry sees that Lena is bleeding. In the blink of an eye he comprehends the imminent threat to everything meaningful in his life. In short order he lays waste to all four brothers from first to last. He even relinquishes his tire-iron to one of them in a gesture of total control. This represents a reversal of the *un*controllable rage he displayed previously — that rage now mastered and channeled into a power he wields selectively. The demonic anger manifested earlier will not appear again for the remainder of the film.

*

In coming to terms with the character of Barry Egan, and his unusual place among Anderson's creations, the film must first be understood in context. Along with 'The Master' (discussed later), 'Punch Drunk Love' is the most unique of all Anderson's films. The dominant role of secular symbolism in preference to biblical points of reference is crucial; but nearly as crucial is the atypical construction of Barry's character from a familial point of view. In nearly all of Anderson's films the main characters are disfigured by parental mistreatment (or absence). This is true for John in 'Hard Eight,' whose father was murdered by Sydney. It's true for Eddie Adams in 'Boogie Nights,' who enjoys no affection from either his shrill mother or distant father. In 'Magnolia,' the dysfunctional relationships between parent and child are almost too numerous to count, contributing to the shattered psychology of nearly every character. Looking forward, the disfigured kinship between Daniel Plainview and H.W. in 'There Will Be Blood' forms a central part of the film's trauma; and in 'The Master' Freddie Quell's parents are either insane or dead, and his new relationship to Lancaster Dodd only compounds his misery. In Anderson's cinema, flawed gods and lost men are the rule rather than the exception.

But Barry *is* the exception. Not only are his mother and father denied any psychological impact on his person, they're never even mentioned in the film. His behavior shows no deformity born of parental dysfunction, rather his emotional difficulty stems from his seven sisters. Granted, this is still familial dysfunction; but the absence of any maternal or paternal malpractice results in a peculiar freedom for Barry — his freedom of will. Unlike so many characters preceding him, he is not defined by the negative psychological imprint of his parents. Indeed, the film suggests nothing of their influence on his motives or actions. Because there exists no such influence, Barry is free to make of himself what he wants.

In Anderson's films, fate itself forms a kind of parental influence because it's rooted in divine intervention. God is the 'parent' in this model; the ultimate father-figure. But in 'Punch Drunk Love' there is no divine symbolism or parental presence. Anderson takes the extreme measure of exorcising any parental influence from the film, be it a mother and father to Barry, or the presence of a divine godhead. There are no flawed gods in the film, period. There is just Barry. His odyssey of discovery is completely self-motivated. His salvation comes in the form of another person, Lena; and his only inspiration comes from the harmonium—an instrument that must be actively played to produce music. In many ways the film itself is a metaphor for the application of human will to produce harmony—Barry finding it within himself to discover, pursue, and harmonize with Lena. He manifests an identity which is born solely of his own self-contained transformation, rooted in his love for one special woman. All of which makes Barry Egan a uniquely powerful figure; perhaps the most powerful creation in any of Anderson's films—particularly because he suffers no personal loss along the way. After Lena is hurt, he becomes unassailable. His love makes him greater than himself; a result of his own determination.

It therefore comes as no surprise that he seeks closure with the Mattress-Man, Dean Trumbell. Their phone conversation is a diatribe which transforms Barry into a tense coil of electricity. In no time at all, still clutching the telephone, Barry appears in the doorway of the Mattress Man's refuge. The scene unfolds like a Western showdown, only here Barry's weapon is the active love in his heart. As they stare each other down, face to face, Barry declares: "I have so much strength in me you have no idea. I have a love in my life that makes me stronger than anything you can imagine." After a moment of hesitation, Dean replies: "You came all the way from L.A. to tell me this." Barry nods, and the Mattress Man relents: "That's that." Instantly Barry reclaims his manhood and secures Lena's safety. Where once he was a victim of circumstance, now he is the maker of his own destiny. The strength of his will, matched to the love he harbors for Lena, redeems him completely.

In the penultimate scene of the film Barry finally acknowledges the great bridge to his awakening: the mysterious harmonium. He takes the instrument—a pillar of strength—into his arms and races to Lena's apartment. There he apologizes for leaving her at the hospital, and inevitably she forgives him. But his insistence on bringing the harmonium into that supremely intimate scene reveals an understanding of its harmony. This human instrument has given him a connection to something he feared he'd never discover: love itself. Over the course of the film his mastery of its harmony is manifested in the love he seeks, and completely attains, from Lena Leonard.

The closing lines of dialogue are among the simplest Anderson has written. They contain truthful declarations, and allow reciprocal resolution between the main characters. Barry finally finds a use for all the pudding he's amassed: he can redeem it for frequent-flier miles to accompany Lena wherever her business takes her: "I can get enough mileage to go with you wherever you have to go, if you have to travel for your work; because I don't ever want to be anywhere without you." It's a moment of emotional courage and vulnerability, animated by the fully requited love they share.

The last line of dialogue, delivered by Lena, is both an end and a beginning. It marks the end of the film and the beginning of their journey through life together, articulated in four simple words: "So here we go." It's the summation of everything the film aspires to say, accompanied by an image of secular trinity: Barry, Lena, and the harmonium. Harmony, love, and light. These are the hallmarks of the film's ending; a declaration of independence lovingly portrayed in red, white, and blue.

Perhaps the most resonant aspect of the film is that it represents Anderson's unshakable commitment to grow his own artistry. His films always bear the imprint of whatever process he happens to be working through, whether it's the pessimism that marked his early shorts, or the optimism that manifests the great rain of frogs in 'Magnolia.' His films are an outgrowth of ideas, animating his own artistic journey. In 'Punch Drunk Love,' Anderson tackles a new mode of representation—not the divine intervention of flawed gods and lost men, but the human quest for fulfillment motivated by one man's will. Further, this new territory is populated by secular, not biblical, symbols. The final result is a product of self-assessment and artistic reaction.

In fact, the basic narrative of 'Punch Drunk Love' would still be plausible without the harmonium. It's not essential to conveying a love story. But Anderson is ambitious. He deliberately fashions a secular symbol to test his desire for new modes of visual depiction. In fact, the harmonium plays so dominant a role in the film precisely because it represents a departure from his previous cinema. From a purely aesthetic point of view, the harmonium is the star of the film. Its mysterious appearance only suits one purpose: to further Anderson's artistry. It is never explained in the narrative, nor was it designed to be.

This passion to explore his artistry on-screen defines Anderson as a filmmaker who constantly pushes his sensibility in new directions. That he never fails to deliver provocative cinema is testament to his instinct. In 'Punch Drunk Love,' the rejection of religious symbolism, together with a minimal visual palette and an emphasis on free will, result in a film which matches his aesthetic proclivity at that particular moment. Understanding Anderson's methods, specifically the incorporation of new ideas into the body of his cinema, will prove a crucial template for interpreting his next work, the colossal 'There Will Be Blood.' In that film more than any other Anderson distills his art into one instance of human conflict. It's also the film which owes the greatest debt of gratitude to the artistic model established in 'Punch Drunk Love,' where biblical imagery and divine influence are replaced by secular symbolism and free will, respectively.

'There Will Be Blood,' goes further still. It gives Anderson the opportunity to strengthen his artistry by building from past successes while proclaiming an aesthetic sense of closure. This process occurs through a symbolic act of annihilation whereby Anderson's chosen protagonist purposely slays a most persistent demon.

Part Five:

THERE WILL BE BLOOD

*

After making 'Hard Eight' in 1996 Anderson only required a year and a half to finish 'Boogie Nights.' After that he spent two years cultivating 'Magnolia.' Then, three years went into the realization of 'Punch Drunk Love.' But in the aftermath of that pivotal film, a full five years were needed to breathe life into his most imposing work, 'There Will Be Blood.' That span of years is greater than the time it took to complete his first three films combined. The issue of that long pregnancy was a creature of immense power; much more physically confrontational than any previous effort. The transformative qualities that distinguish 'Punch Drunk Love' from Anderson's earlier films spawned in him a new thematic approach to his writing. Further, they inspired a material reinvention of his symbolic vocabulary. So strong were these creative impulses that 'There Will Be Blood,' above all else, represents Anderson's effort to stage a battle for his own artistic survival.

Begin with the groundwork. First and foremost Anderson chose a story set in the past. 'There Will Be Blood' traces a period between 1898 and 1927, stopping just short of the Great Depression. This would mark the first ever period-piece he attempted. Moreover, he based the screenplay on a contemporary novel, Upton Sinclair's 'Oil!' instead of developing an original screenplay. This too would mark a first; here fulfilling a very specific purpose. Lastly he chose two very distinct, opposing themes to represent the film's ideological struggle: the sacred and profane.

The film begins not with image, but with sound. The terse strings of Jonny Greenwood's handsome score flood the screen as the camera opens on a California desert in 1898. Immediately the focus is placed on the film's hero, Daniel Plainview. It is difficult to describe the level of electricity Daniel Day Lewis brings to this magnificent figure. From the first shot he's an incarnation of sheer will and locomotion, hammering into the walls of a silver-mine. Cinematically, these opening images are a validation of the medium, expressing the character's tenacity against element and earth entirely through visual means. Only one word is uttered in the first fourteen minutes of the film, and that is barely a gasp. Anderson constructs an ominous chain of images that depict a man obsessed with finding his fortune; a man who would forego his own health and well-being—even his own sanity—to reap mineral wealth.

Daniel Plainview is not a man who kneels before fate. Rather he's a creature of human will, very different from the type of character Anderson tends to introduce at the start of his films. Think of John in 'Hard Eight,' Dirk in 'Boogie Nights,' Officer Jim in 'Magnolia,' and Barry Egan in 'Punch Drunk Love.' All of these characters depended on external motivation or divine coincidence at the outset. But Daniel embodies the polar-opposite of externally determined motive.

He's a man who shapes his own fortune; who does not wait for fate to deal him a winning (or losing) hand. This is crucial to interpreting the film, for Anderson is crafting something deliberately primordial: a struggle which pits two symbolic figures—two archetypes—in a fight to the death. To that end he purposely arms his symbolic hero, Daniel Plainview, with the will of a conqueror.

Anderson's decision to begin the film on Daniel's effort to draw raw silver from the earth sets the tone. His aggressive digging represents Anderson's effort to reap cinematic profit from himself. He carefully lays the groundwork for a mining of his own sensibility in the name of artistic growth. His high standards of creativity—which constantly dig into new ideas, evolving themes, and renewed symbols—imply a strong aversion to aesthetic stagnation. For him it's not enough to simply make movies; each film should represent an attempt to express a more perfect vision than before.

The benefit of this self-imposed standard is fairly obvious when his films are assessed chronologically. For example, the level of artistic sophistication in 'There Will Be Blood' is higher than that of, say, 'Hard Eight' or 'Boogie Nights.' This is true both on a visual and ideological level. Anderson's own yardstick demands a constant elevation of cinematic expression. Any hindrance to that growth may be considered a threat to his survival as a filmmaker. And that's why, in the body of this film, P. T. Anderson conceives an extraordinarily purposeful design. He fashions a protagonist, embodied by Daniel Plainview, for one purpose only: to annihilate a burdensome arch-symbol. That symbol, so long a staple of his art, is divine intervention. Here, Eli Sunday, an ambitious preacher whom Daniel meets at the end of the first act, represents that towering, nagging, icon.

This lone objective explains why Anderson was so drawn to the source material in the first place. Sinclair's novel is somewhat stuffy, and lends little to the finished film. But it does revolve around unique themes which coincide with Anderson's artistic interests at this time. First, it allows him to set the film in the past. This is imperative because the movie is an exercise in confrontation—here the director confronting his own artistic past. As discussed, his early sensibility centers on a particular kind of fateful encounter; namely divine intervention. That motif dominates Anderson's first three films and even casts a shadow over his fourth. 'In Punch Drunk Love' however, he stages a coup which temporarily severs his allegiance to biblical symbolism. Doing so grants him liberation, which in turn fosters a new impulse in his creative direction. Anderson now faced a fork in the road; a struggle between two artistic paths: one leading to previous modes of expression (i.e. divine intervention), the other leading to something undiscovered. That struggle to choose the right path between past and future is manifested directly in 'There Will Be Blood,' and quite rightly the title is an apt description of the film's inevitable resolution.

So, in the aftermath of building 'Punch Drunk Love' around secular symbols, Anderson had a choice: continue using biblical points of reference (divine intervention) as a template for his films; or embrace the more abstract, secular modes of representation that worked so well in that fourth film. For Anderson, whose artistry seeks growth and progression, the choice was clear. It was also difficult. Difficult because the level of artistic achievement in his first three films was so high; and Anderson could not be certain his new devotion to secular symbolism would prove as successful. But again, because he makes certain demands of himself, he chose the more challenging artistic path. The return to the past embodied in 'There Will Be Blood' is thus a depiction of the artist delving into his own past to confront his creative demons. To that end he builds Daniel Plainview into a purposeful executioner. For Anderson, the film represents a declaration of war that naturally follows his declaration of independence in 'Punch Drunk Love.' Here, however, the stakes are much higher.

Beyond the setting of Sinclair's novel it's important to note the symbolism borrowed from the book. First is the oil itself. Throughout 'There Will Be Blood,' iron derricks tower over the insignificant people of the town. They're man-made giants; symbols of capitalist greed and human domination. Indeed, oil itself promotes power through mechanization. The product of decomposed life, oil is not inherently valuable. It is only valuable because men have tailored it to the machines of commerce and war. To control this substance is to command the mechanized world – and by extension to command other men. This symbol suits Anderson's desire to tether his hero, in no uncertain terms, to the secular universe. Daniel Plainview is that powerful hero.

Opposing him is the symbol of divinity, here personified by the strange figure of Eli Sunday. He's a master preacher; a man of God whose great concern is the salvation of his flock through the Church of the Third Revelation. As the competing power in the narrative, his armaments are the traditional icons of religion: the crucifix, the church, and the strength of holy ritual. In the figure of Eli Sunday, Anderson invests every remnant of divine intervention and religious symbolism from his previous films. By contrast, he collects everything he understands of the secular universe — everything anti-religious — in the figure of Daniel Plainview. The murderous struggle between them, physically and ideologically, is the centerpiece of the film. It is Anderson's attempt to chart a new course for his artistry. By empowering Daniel Plainview to defeat his competitor — his obstacle — he makes a willful decision to master his aesthetic domain. Daniel's destruction of Eli Sunday in the final scene thus represents a very personal artistic gesture; one in which Anderson breaks the yoke of divine symbolism so persistently guiding his work.

About twenty minutes into the film (the year 1911) a soft-spoken messenger, Paul Sunday, enters Daniel's place of business to bring him tidings of prosperity. For a small sum he reveals to Daniel the location of a great reserve of oil; a vast ocean of wealth. Daniel is suspicious of the boy but eventually follows his mysterious lead. Paul leaves, never to be seen again. Before long Daniel and his adopted son, H.W., arrive at the Sunday Ranch in Little Boston, California. The meeting between Paul (who may be a reference to St. Paul, Christianity's most important messenger) and Daniel is almost certainly a motivating example of divine intervention. However, once Daniel arrives at the Sunday Ranch he remains a total embodiment of human will. He soon meets Paul's brother, Eli, an even more potent symbol of divinity. Almost immediately a power struggle manifests between the two. Daniel will come to represent a curse upon Eli, one made all the more ironic given that Eli's own brother delivered it.

The Sunday Ranch does in fact sit on a pool of oil. In negotiating a purchase of the land Daniel opens a dialogue with Abel, the patriarch, and Eli himself. It quickly becomes apparent that Eli is no fool, demanding much more for the land than Daniel was planning to pay. Here Eli disrupts the arbitration which might make Daniel a wealthy man. He intervenes in his business—literally making himself an instrument of divine intervention. At this point his motive is not supernatural; rather it's material. He secures a greater price for the ranch only because he wants to enlarge his church.

This intervention on Eli's part is minor compared to the grand gestures Anderson devised for previous films, and it reveals the low regard he holds for divine symbolism by this time in his artistic development. It's worth noting that Eli does not alter the trajectory of Daniel's will here—the land is still purchased, merely at an inflated price. On top of that, Daniel never makes good on the promissory payment to Eli's church. Anderson is already allocating a greater cunning and instinct to Daniel, and this imbalance will only grow as the film moves forward.

A brief overview of the differences between Upton Sinclair's 'Oil!' and 'There Will Be Blood' is warranted because the alterations reveal Anderson's willingness to borrow only the best thematic material in shaping his own work. In the book, the central protagonist is named J.A. Ross, an oil entrepreneur. He's assisted by his son, J.A. Ross Jr., affectionately referred to as 'Bunny.' Ross Sr. is a realist, and runs his business in a manner that reflects the rigor of the industry. He takes what he wants, and makes little apology. His son, whose insight forms the narrative of the novel, begins to see the error of his father's ways. More importantly he sees the error of Capitalism itself (especially the manner by which labor is exploited for profit). Ross Sr., like Daniel Plainview, buys a parcel of land from a local family, although in the book their name is Watkins, not Sunday. The patriarch of that family has two sons, Paul and Eli; and the latter does indeed become an influential preacher. Paul, by contrast, becomes a Socialist and a mentor to young Bunny. There is no character in the book to parallel Henry, who claims to be Daniel's brother in the film. And there is no bad blood between Ross Sr. and Eli in the book. Sinclair treats them not as enemies, but rather as two sides of the same corrupt coin. Lastly, the biological relationship between Bunny and his father is strong throughout the novel, and at no time does Bunny suffer a loss of hearing.

Now, Anderson could have fashioned a straight adaptation of the book, probably with good results. But again, this is an artist of ambition who seeks constant growth within the medium. It's not surprising that his adaptation is selective. His interest principally lies in Sinclair's thematic competition between religious and secular power. Anderson extracts that dynamic from the novel and forges it into something much more deadly. Changing the family name to 'Sunday' indicates his effort to underscore the contrast between these two competing powers. Choosing the name 'Plainview' over 'Ross' for the opposing force only heightens that contrast. Further, Anderson enlarges the role of Eli in the film, making him the sole symbol of religious ambition. Paul is dismissed altogether; his presence unnecessary to the one-on-one struggle Anderson intends to pursue. The relationship between Daniel and H.W. is also very different from that between Ross Sr. and Bunny. Anderson prefers the theme of paternal disharmony, which informs so much of his work. To that end he makes H.W. the adopted son of Daniel Plainview. This fractured and diminished relationship allows a more devastating sense of family tragedy by the end of the film; leaving Daniel both physically and emotionally isolated.

Anderson makes these alterations for one simple reason: he intends to tell a precise story about the struggle between two competing powers; none of which requires a multitude of political intrigue. In fact, despite its epic scale and imposing figures, 'There Will Be Blood' presents the same minimal narrative that defined 'Punch Drunk Love.' Like that effort, the film centers on two characters and the dynamic that joins them. 'In Punch Drunk Love,' that dynamic was harmony. Here, it's *dis*harmony. This carefully devised power-struggle represents Anderson's own struggle for artistic mastery.

*

Throughout the film Anderson seems driven to surpass his own high standards. Every facet of his visual composition glows diamond bright with detail. Great western deserts fill the lens, splitting the frame into two horizontal halves dominated by blue sky above and brown earth below. The texture of the film burns with oil and blood. Risen metal siphons the earth; scorched, sun-hot, hissing with flame.

Anderson himself is a product of the West. He knows its temporal beauty; its raw wind and rare rain. To depict a land of such elemental turbulence he thrusts his camera into darkened wells, presses it into the brows of fearful men, and scans long swaths of virgin earth. Matching Anderson's vision measure for measure is the harrowing score by Jonny Greenwood. A spare reflection of the film's internal landscape, Greenwood's strings express moments of austerity and sacrifice. The visual world is Anderson's, but Greenwood should be credited for much of the film's aural anguish.

The players too exhibit a rare kinship with this rough environment. The subtle temptation that informs Paul Dano's vocal inflections, the muscular control of Daniel Day-Lewis' frenetic commands, and the frail pity in Kevin O'Conner's depiction of Henry, all point to a cast who willingly transport themselves to a primal past. They lend physical gravity to the film, digging down to scour their demons even as Anderson seeks to purge his own. Perhaps in no other film does he display so sure a sense of symphony, best exemplified by the visual crescendo which marks the first eruption of the Sunday well.

In the middle of the film (so often the point where things go wrong), Anderson unleashes the most spectacular visual event in any of his films: the eruption of an oil derrick into a demonic pillar of flame. It's an image that roars with savagery, both wildly uncontainable and beautifully mesmerizing. The adjoining score is a scream of fury, pulsing with percussive echoes. Anderson directs the ritual with terrific frenzy, using the camera to track the crew's flailing efforts to quell the fire. It's as if Anderson was filming a colony of ants whose mound had just been blown by an unseen force.

At the center of the eruption, H.W. is injured. Daniel rushes to save the boy; Anderson's camera follows close. Around and around the workers scurry to control the fall of the derrick—the anti-god symbol bathed in flames. Through the wreckage Daniel discerns the miracle of the moment, proclaiming to his associate: "What are you looking so miserable about? There's a whole ocean of oil under our feet, and no one can get at it except for me!" His palpable excitement is only minimally diminished when the associate asks: "Is H.W. all right?" and Daniel stoically responds: "No, he isn't." But he can't turn his focus from the well. The oil is his love; his reason for living. Above all, this staggering scene reveals Daniel's superhuman passion for mastering the material world. Anderson too must feel this passion—for mastering his medium.

H.W.'s sudden loss of hearing—a result of the well's eruption—poses a tremendous emotional conflict for Daniel. On the one hand he seems to love the boy; and clearly regards him as a kind of heir. In their many years of wrangling, Daniel has always kept H.W. close beside him. On the other hand, it can be argued that H.W. is simply a prop which allows Daniel to maintain the façade of family life and religious value. Early in the film, a key scene reveals Daniel lying about the boy's mother, citing her supposed death during child-birth. "It's just me and my son now," he declares; lending some credence to the 'prop' argument.

However, this criticism fails to explain the sincere emotional expression Daniel manifests for his son. If he was only interested in H.W. as a prop, then why shed tears during private moments? Why exhibit conflicted feelings? Indeed, once the valuable Sunday property is purchased and the first oil-well built, Daniel is free to dispense with the boy however he likes. Why bother with another mouth to feed, now that his purpose has been served? But instead he keeps H.W. close to him, both physically and emotionally, until the sad day when he sends him to a boarding school. And even this doesn't occur until H.W. attempts to burn down the cabin where his father sleeps.

Conflicted feelings aside, it eventually becomes clear that H.W. represents a burden to Daniel. The film does not shy away from Daniel's irritation at having to live with his son's crippled hearing. The daily catering to H.W.'s needs becomes oppressive to Daniel, and his increasing distaste for these chores foments a growing emotional detachment. In turn, this promotes feelings of abandonment in H.W. This dynamic between father and son, so deep and binding, is one that Anderson comprehends well. In this instance it's made more complex by virtue of the fact that H.W. is not Daniel's biological son. He is adopted; which creates a further schism within Daniel. Inevitably he sends the boy away, but not without intense emotional remorse (revealed during his later baptism into the Church of the Third Revelation).

Meanwhile Daniel has come to revile Eli Sunday and everything he stands for. In an earlier scene he witnesses the exorcism of a 'devil' from a woman attending Eli's church. Old and frail, she suffers from arthritis. Eli looms over her, twisting and hissing in a fit of gross contortion to expel the demon from her body. The display is both primitive and serpentine, possessing ominous implication. Daniel tells him later: "That was one goddamn hell of a show," making it clear he doesn't believe this charade for one minute. But Daniel is aware of the uncommon reverence allotted this preacher by the community. Eli is influential and respected. He's seen by many as a spiritual prophet. This makes him a threat in Daniel's eyes—or more accurately, a competitor. His distaste for Eli finally turns to hatred after H.W. loses his hearing. If Eli can expel demons and heal the sick, why doesn't he heal H.W.? This is the thrust of Daniel's loathing of Eli; instilling within him a rage for this false-prophet and his carnival theatrics.

In a key scene, set near a pool of oil, Eli approaches Daniel about the money he's owed. The result is the first instance where Daniel physically dominates Eli. He slaps him hard across the face, punishing him relentlessly. It's an explosive release of primal rage which doesn't cease until Eli has been nearly smothered to death. The symbolism is quite striking. Daniel stuffs handfuls of thick oil into Eli's screaming face, larding him in black gold. The sheer power unleashed against Eli proves euphoric. Daniel takes delight in humiliating this agent of divine intervention—itself an act that Anderson directs. Daniel comes close to suffocating Eli once and for all, boldly declaring: "I'm going to bury you underground!" But Anderson, who understands the construction of tragedy, jealously harbors that moment for the film's powerfully cathartic ending.

One aspect of the film which owes nothing to the novel is the introduction of a disheveled character named Henry. This man meets Daniel outside his cabin and claims to be his long-lost brother. The story he tells, of being destitute after failing to find silver in New Mexico, is believable because facets of his story convey information that only a brother could know. In short order he gains Daniel's confidence, agreeing to work with him until such time that he can save a little money and move on. The arrival of a close family member — importantly a blood relative — provides an unexpected comfort to Daniel, who tells Henry in a moment of rare vulnerability: "Having you here gives me a second breath."

It's crucial to remember that H.W. is adopted. Thus, for Daniel, the arrival of a biological sibling returns a real sense of familial connection to his life. Up to this point his closest confidant was H.W., whom he treated as a legitimate son. But after H.W. loses his hearing, Daniel finds it difficult to maintain his parental façade. H.W. can't hear him, can't absorb his wisdom — rather he just eats and sleeps. In many ways, H.W. becomes little more than a pet to Daniel. But with Henry's arrival comes a sense of reawakening. Daniel now believes he can pass along his wealth of knowledge to a true blood relative; someone he knows he can trust. This idea of replacement — Henry for H.W. — is finally realized when H.W. sets fire to the cabin where Daniel and his brother sleep. In the cruel aftermath Daniel sends him to a boarding school; a decision made easier because he now has a brother to fill the emotional gap.

In fact, Daniel becomes so close to Henry that he shares some very personal thoughts with him; sullen feelings that dwell within his troubled soul. Alone together, he initiates a measured sequence of dialogue: "Are you an angry man, Henry? Are you envious? Do you get envious? I have a competition in me. I want no one else to succeed. . . There are times when I look at people and I see nothing worth liking." Daniel's admission here suggests the absolute trust he places in Henry. The speech also reveals the darker aspects of his character. This is a man who makes no allowance for those of meager strength or savvy. The real irony is Daniel's own lack of savvy. He invests his full faith and confidence in a total imposter.

In this secret utterance one almost discerns the voice of Anderson as well; cautiously articulating his own dark side. Perhaps the 'competition' Daniel refers to is the competition within the filmmaker himself; purposely established to further his art. Here the competitor is divine intervention, manifested in the figure of Eli Sunday. This is the obstacle — the hindrance to Anderson's growth — that must be destroyed. The private dialogue in this scene possesses a most personal inflection; one that exemplifies Anderson's pursuit of truthful art through vulnerable expose´. In these words Daniel seems to reveal Anderson as a driven, competitive artist. Perhaps in that revelation lies the source of his success.

Unfortunately, Daniel's trust in Henry goes unrewarded. In a foreboding scene they sit together on a sunny beach, reminiscing over old memories. Daniel mentions a house he once adored; a house he wanted to own, be married in, let children run through. Henry listens, and nods. He suggests they enjoy a drink later; maybe get some women. To which Daniel responds, in an wry moment of nostalgia: "Take 'em to the Peachtree dance." Henry is unmoved by the remark, merely smiling along. Daniel repeats the phrase: "I say, get liquored up and take 'em to the Peachtree dance." Henry simply returns the same vague smile: "Yeah." In that instant lies his doom. The reference is obviously meaningful; a memory that Daniel knows neither could forget. In the next frame he shakes his head in disbelief.

He realizes this 'brother' is a liar, and that he, Daniel, has been played for a fool. Anderson shrewdly hides Henry in a dark swathe of shadow as Daniel dives back into the ocean to cleanse his body of the filthy discovery. Soon after, in the dead of night, Daniel confronts his so-called brother. When his suspicions are confirmed, he murders Henry in cold blood.

This gruesome scene marks the first instance where Daniel commits murder. In displaying this facet of his character, Anderson lays the groundwork for Daniel's ultimate act of destruction at the end of the film. Here the factor that determines Henry's death is his intolerable deception. It is the fulcrum upon which Daniel's wrathful actions pivot. He will not suffer betrayal; he will not be made into an ass. He concludes that the lie, and the liar, must be punished. The death-sentence which follows is thus motivated by vengeance — for the lies Henry told and the trust he falsely cultivated. All of which points to the manner by which the greatest of all liars, Eli Sunday, will finally meet his end.

To a great extent Daniel's understanding of family unity hinges on loyalty. That loyalty was always present in H.W. even if his adopted status compromised the truth of their biological relationship. When H.W. loses his hearing, that loyalty is disrupted because Daniel cannot connect with his son. So, after sending him away, Daniel places his emotional investment in Henry — and now that relationship is disrupted too. Henry betrays Daniel, leaving him no one to trust; no one to inherit his empire. The emotional toll exacted by this denial of kinship (and denial of truth) affects Daniel profoundly. It leaves him more vulnerable than ever. He once had a loving son and a loyal brother; now he has neither. His darkest days are just beginning.

This is Daniel's emotional mindset as he's baptized into the Church of the Third Revelation. He does not participate willingly, but he must endure it if he's to gain William Bandy's permission to run a pipeline through his property. Daniel desperately needs this pipeline; his entire fortune depends on it. So in a scene brimming with emotional catharsis, Daniel suffers the judgment of the man he loathes. Eli Sunday forces Daniel to his knees and makes him say the things he fears most: "I am a sinner! I've abandoned my child! I've abandoned my boy!" In forcing Daniel to do his bidding, Eli represents the symbol of divinity that looms over Anderson himself. Indeed, the confrontation here is a metaphor for Anderson's struggle to accept divine intervention—allow it into his art—just as Daniel is forced to accept Christ. The composition is entirely one-sided, with Eli towering over Daniel's submissive figure. The latter vomits up a deep confession, purging his sin. The scene proceeds as a visual manifestation of 'reckoning' through which Daniel confesses his past transgressions, suffers humility, and accepts his punishment. The process is designed to foster spiritual growth in Daniel (and by extension, artistic growth in Anderson). Above all this sequence reveals the director's total devotion to the medium; willfully transposing his inner-turmoil to the screen.

*

As the narrative moves toward resolution, Anderson brings all the principals back onto the stage. He begins by returning H.W. to Daniel. It's not a coincidence that he returns only after the emotional confession in the previous scene; but H.W. is very different now. He lacks emotional trust for his father, slapping Daniel almost as soon as they're reunited. Confusing matters greatly is the introduction of a new figure: a teacher of the deaf who instructs H.W. in sign-language. This is another symbolic turn of events where one character is 'replaced' by another. Earlier Henry replaced H.W. in Daniel's familial universe. Now, ironically, Daniel himself is replaced by this unnamed instructor. Suddenly *he* becomes the man who understands H.W., who speaks and listens to him. Despite their physical proximity, Daniel and H.W. are no closer than they were during the boy's absence. Indeed, so foreign is their relationship that H.W. now speaks an altogether different language. Sadly, Daniel makes no attempt to learn it, further removing himself from H.W.'s emotional sphere.

The introduction of sign-language into the film has a symbolic purpose coinciding with Anderson's intent to isolate his protagonist. Daniel can't communicate with his son anymore. By extension Anderson implies that, in fact, he can't communicate with anyone. He doesn't speak any language but his own; he's become removed and reclusive. To a certain extent sign-language is a metaphor for the new 'language' of the film as well. 'There Will Be Blood' represents a number of 'firsts' for Anderson. It's his first period-film. It's the first time he uses an adapted script. Eli Sunday is the first openly religious figure in any of his movies. And for the first time the concept of free will, through Daniel, is embraced from the very beginning. All of these examples signal a reconceived artistic language that communicates new vitality.

One shot in particular summarizes Anderson's embrace of new artistic models. In the last scene before the final act, H.W., still just a boy, leaps from a platform. Mary Sunday follows after; both merely playing. The scene depicts a wonderful leap of faith that inevitably leads to marriage. And just as H.W. and Mary take that leap to a greater place, so too does Anderson's filmmaking find new promise through the artistic leap the film represents.

Anderson sets the final act of the narrative in 1927. He begins it with the marriage of H.W. and Mary, and ends it with the murder of Eli Sunday. This framing device, modulating from blissful union to fatal separation, exemplifies the wide thematic span traversed through the course of the film. H.W.'s marriage also conveys a common theme in Anderson's art: the incarnation of hope from tragedy through requited love. Here, perhaps more so than any previous film, the final act depicts a Pandora's box in which H.W.'s marriage embodies a quiet optimism. Beneath even that, on an interpretive level, the real emerging hope is Anderson's art.

But first Anderson must clear the deck. The sole purpose of the film is to present a focused conflict between two characters: Daniel and Eli. To do this he must remove every peripheral figure from the stage. He begins by sundering the relationship between Daniel and his son. By now Daniel's health has deteriorated greatly. He is the product of intense physical hardship, weary from the strain of battling his way to the top. When H.W. arrives to see him, he's emotionally disfigured as well. Neither has done much to bridge the widening gap between them. Significantly, Daniel made no effort to attend H.W.'s wedding (or wasn't invited), and this only deepens their estrangement. Now H.W. makes one last attempt to gain his father's blessing. He's unaware their relationship hangs by the barest thread—one Daniel willingly severs when pressed into a spiteful corner.

H.W. announces that he wants to become an oil man, intent on establishing a drilling operation with his wife in Mexico. Instead of congratulating his son, Daniel receives this news as a grave betrayal. In his mind, H.W. is trying to hurt him—even humiliate him—just as Henry hurt him with his charade of brotherhood and Eli humiliated him with his carnival baptism. Now his own son seeks to harm him with a direct threat of competition. For Daniel this is no cause for celebration, rather it's another instance of disloyalty and untruthfulness. He's so emotionally hollow by this point that he can only view people as friend or foe. H.W. is now a foe. Their exchange instantly calls to mind his earlier words to Henry: "I have a competition in me. I want no one else to succeed." Calcifying his state of mind is the hard emotional wall he's built around himself. No one may enter this domain, not even a loved one. The volatility here is white-hot, portending the release of violent emotions.

Like Frank T.J. Mackie, Daniel won't allow pain to consume him. In the blink of an eye he decides to inflict more emotional ruin on others than they can inflict on him. Tragically, the object of his scorn is his own son. He reveals to

H.W. that, in fact, he's not his son at all. He's an orphan, adopted like an animal from the wild. Daniel's declaration bristles with malice: "You're an orphan from a basket in the middle of the desert. You have none of me in you, you're someone else's. . . I took you in for no other reason than I needed a sweet face to buy land. You're *lower* than a bastard." H.W. measures every word — emotionally confused at first — then manages to hold strong: "I thank God I have none of you in me." He leaves, even as Daniel's denunciation floods the cavernous hallway: "Bastard from a basket!"

Despite Daniel's effort to hurt his son, it's he who suffers most. His venomous curse is not enough to quell his own pain. Again, like T.J. Mackie, his carefully constructed defense mechanism fails. H.W.'s departure severs an important tie, leaving Daniel one step closer to emotional despair. However this total isolation is important to Daniel's ultimate resurrection. He must lose everything if he's to be redeemed; he must suffer absolute abandonment by those he once loved. There's an element of the biblical story of Job here, but turned inside-out. Daniel — and by extension Anderson — will be redeemed not by the acceptance of divinity, but by its total annihilation. To this end, there will be blood.

The last scene represents the final confrontation between Anderson's chosen hero (embodied by Daniel) and the figure of divine symbolism (embodied by Eli). Just as divinity so often loomed over Anderson's art, so too does Eli now loom over Daniel's semi-conscious body in the bowling alley of his dreadful mansion. This is the setting of a murder — an act both destructive and regenerative at the same time; the ultimate resolution. By destroying a flawed god, Daniel will reap his salvation.

As he did before the murder of Henry, Daniel first insists on a confession. He approaches the edge of reason, drunk with power, playing his foe like a mastered instrument. Eli informs him that William Bandy has died, and that his coveted land is now available for drilling. Daniel feigns great interest in purchasing the land from Eli, but on one condition: Eli must declare that he is a false-prophet and that God is a superstition. Here Daniel seeks to exact upon Eli the same humiliation that Eli evoked from him in the baptism scene. Daniel adds irony to the composition: he makes Eli stand up, placing him above Daniel spatially, in order to recreate their relative positions in that earlier episode. Eli then repeats over and over, louder and louder: "I am a false prophet, God is a superstition!" Meanwhile Daniel calmly eats his steak, nourishing himself as Eli speaks. On another level, it's Anderson who nourishes himself by confronting his own demon through the film. He takes pleasure in humiliating this greatly diminished symbol; draining its power even as he empowers himself.

Anderson constructs this scene as the capstone of the narrative; the moment where he destroys Eli Sunday and what he represents. In 'Punch Drunk Love,' Anderson made a conscious choice to subtract divine influence from the film as a motivating symbol. Here he takes the next logical step: he annihilates it completely. Artistically, this would suggest a total break from utilizing biblical points of reference; however his next film does not hew to this notion. Indeed, 'The Master' poses a unique interpretive challenge; one almost wholly dependent on the war waged in this monumental work. For now, Anderson's immediate struggle is embodied in the confrontation between Daniel and Eli.

When Eli's confession is finished, Daniel informs him that in fact Bandy's land is totally barren. He drained the oil beneath it many years ago. It's gone, and there's nothing Eli can do about it. This exchange, so aggressively one-sided, shows Daniel's absolute lack of mercy or restraint in leveling his sentence. To destroy this flawed god, Eli must confess his lies, abandon his maker, and accept his punishment. Like Henry and H.W. before him, Eli suffers Daniel's wrath — the judgment of an anti-god. With nowhere to run, Daniel corners him beneath a flood of white light and pulverizes his skull with the hammer-blow of a bowling pin. Not just once, but many times, burying his head into the floor until a pool of blood spreads like an oil-spill. The image seems to echo the chant of Eli's congregation during Daniel's baptism: "You will never be saved if you reject the blood!"

In that instant, Anderson himself is resurrected from the ashes. His art is the hope that emerges from this Pandora's box. Divine intervention, the false-prophet so omniscient in his body of work, is eradicated in the most fatal manner possible. Anderson's chosen protagonist smothers his demon and transcends the act to a greater, more artistically perfect, reward. Indeed the last shot depicts an unabashed triumph of the will as Daniel declares the film's final words. With his back to the audience (indicating private expression) he smiles secretly: "I'm finished."

The great irony of this utterance, spoken amid death, is that Anderson's aesthetic sensibility is very much alive. Little wonder then that he ends the film with the same celebratory music that accompanied the inauguration of Daniel's well much earlier: the final movement of Brahms' Violin Concerto. This is valedictory music meant to heighten feelings of triumph and ascension. That Anderson concludes the film with this magnificent movement underscores his artistic command at this precise moment in his life.

The unique construction of 'There Will Be Blood,' in which Anderson charges a purposeful hero with the task of annihilating an ideological obstacle — almost entering the film himself to do so — resonates with echoes of Shakespeare's 'The Tempest.' In that late play, Prospero acts as Shakespeare's vessel, proclaiming to the audience at the end: "As you from crimes would pardoned be, let your indulgence set me free." Here, Anderson too is set free by the viewer's indulgence. We pardon Daniel's crime of murder for the sake of Anderson's growth as an artist. His next film, 'The Master,' poses an interpretive challenge given the symbolic pronouncement in 'There Will Be Blood.' But the very cause of that film's difficulties derive from the traumatic war waged here. Indeed, in many ways the main characters in Anderson's next film mirror Daniel and Eli. The post-war setting is a remnant of their fatal conflict; the disfigured players moving through it represent human uncertainty in the wake of war.

Part Six:

THE MASTER

*

'The Master' is almost certainly Anderson's most difficult film. Not difficult in the sense of interpretation or classification within his major canon, but rather in its refusal to grant emotional solace or resolution to any of its principal characters. Added to this tone of emptiness is the director's preference for abstraction and violence, which lends a disorienting severity to the film. For the first time in any of his movies (excluding his experimental shorts) Anderson denies any character—principal or peripheral—a path to personal redemption or requited love. In this way the film stands apart, eschewing Anderson's prior commitment to finding stability for his characters through emotional closure. 'The Master' is a dark vision; one that most closely resembles— aesthetically and spiritually—a purgatory.

An informed interpretation of 'The Master' requires a familiarity with the source inspiration for the film, as well as a working knowledge of the major themes that make up Anderson's body of work. To begin, 'The Master' owes much of its origin to John Ford's documentary 'Let There Be Light' (1945), which graphically illustrates the psychological hardships faced by returning servicemen after World War II. This, in turn, forms the basis for 'The Master's' post-war setting and general tone of instability. Ford's documentary highlights the emotional trauma experienced by soldiers during wartime and the baggage they bring home. 'The Master' too places great emphasis on themes of emotional and mental devastation; imposing upon its main character, Freddie Quell, a profound disorientation. This is arguably Anderson's most unbalanced protagonist; a man whose very behavior is shaped by shell-shock. Violence makes up a big part of his defense mechanism; his volatility made all the more dangerous by virtue of its unpredictability. Lancaster Dodd, the 'Master' in the film, often reminds his followers that men stand far above the animal kingdom. Freddie however cannot seem to escape or suppress his animal urges, reduced to them by the trauma of war.

It's also important to consider 'The Master' in context to Anderson's six major films. It's not difficult to find common themes, narrative devices, and character portrayals throughout his work. 'Boogie Nights' and 'Magnolia' share a penchant for massive casts and large-scale panorama. Conversely, 'Hard Eight' and 'Punch Drunk Love' share a more intimate, small-scale preference for stories of love and redemption. Like these couplings, 'The Master' too matches well with another film: the murderous 'There Will Be Blood.' These two films—more than any other pairing—exhibit a 'cause and effect' relationship. To fully understand 'The Master' one must first understand its predecessor; just as an appreciation of any veteran's hardship requires a comprehension of the war he fought.

In assessing 'The Master,' it becomes critical to deconstruct Anderson's 'war' beyond the literal sense. More important is the concept of war, and how it forms the backdrop for the story Anderson wants to tell. 'The Master' is not a war movie in the strict sense. Rather it is concerned with the *aftermath* of war (drawing a parallel with Martin Scorsese's 'Taxi Driver'). Freddie Quell wanders through a post-war setting; but what war? And what does Freddie represent? Ostensibly, he's a returning veteran of World War II. But on a more abstract level Freddie represents the human spirit emerging from, and damaged by, warfare. In the context of Anderson's films then, 'The Master' represents the aftermath of the war waged in 'There Will Be Blood.' Specifically, the violent battle between Daniel Plainview and Eli Sunday, which in fact proves deadly. The end of that film erupts in blood and murder. Its overwhelming theme is victory through mass destruction. As outlined in the previous chapter, this conflict between Daniel and Eli symbolized the very personal war waged by Anderson against his own artistic demons. On a deeper level then, 'The Master' is Anderson's own post-war experience. It represents his own emergence from an emotionally and intellectually draining conflict.

It cannot be easy to create the massive, impactful films that Anderson continually brings to the screen. The making of these films must be exhaustive, requiring every ounce of commitment both physically and mentally (not to mention the inspiration required to write the scripts). 'There Will Be Blood' is arguably Anderson's most brutal achievement. It manifests a war between two titanic symbols; finding closure only through murder. Undoubtedly the experience proved draining to the artist. In the aftermath, Anderson then naturally gravitated to a narrative that wanders through post-war uncertainty, shell-shock, and the emotional limbo that exists in the wake of war. Freddie Quell is a deeply sympathetic character to Anderson; and in telling his story the director invests some of himself—and his past—in that shattered figure. Jimmy Gator's phrase from 'Magnolia' again reverberates here: 'The Book says we might be through with the past, but the past ain't through with us.'

Anderson falls back upon an often used theme in 'The Master,' one grotesquely embodied in the strange figure of Lancaster Dodd. He represents a flawed god, and by extension, divine intervention. As the leader of a cult known as 'The Cause,' his influence over Freddie forms the basis of a dysfunctional relationship. Their encounter comes entirely by chance, and it proves much less rewarding than any similar dynamic portrayed in Anderson's previous films. In fact, this raises a key question: Why does Anderson again conjure a flawed god to motivate the protagonist in the film—especially given the annihilation of Eli Sunday in 'There Will Be Blood?' Isn't this yet another instance where a young, relatively naïve character is brought under the tutelage of an older, more charismatic father-figure? Isn't Lancaster Dodd simply a different incarnation of Sydney, or Jack Horner? Here, the answers are tied to the post-war setting of the film.

It's not that Anderson is content to recycle old themes, nor does he return to previous archetypes simply because he understands them. Rather the choice to construct a fateful relationship between young man and old master serves a very deliberate purpose. Namely, that in the aftermath of war uncertainty prevails—psychological and emotional un-certainty that results in a yearning for known sources of comfort, however abusive those sources might be. That's why Anderson's old demons—flawed gods and lost men—appear yet again. This same craving for comfort also explains why alcohol plays so prominent a role in the film. That numbing substance represents a false comfort for Freddie; a temporary escape that symbolizes his inability to find clear direction. Liquor further represents the mental disorientation that accompanies the physical upheaval of post-war trauma. Like alcohol, Lancaster Dodd too provides Freddie false guidance. But war has deprived Freddie of sure footing. It has instilled in him feelings of helplessness, and a desire for familiarity and comfort—blinding him to the negative qualities *of* that comfort. Freddie is not unlike a battered wife, or abused pet. He doesn't possess the psychological strength to understand his situation because war has disfigured his judgment.

So, by again relying on this dynamic of 'flawed gods and lost men' to tell the story of Freddie Quell, Anderson himself assumes the veteran's trauma and 'returns home' to something known. In the wake of war, the uneasy search for some source of comfort brings Anderson back to his old demons (compounding the notion that war itself is haunting presence). Because Lancaster Dodd is so decisive, so confident, so masterful, it becomes all too easy for Freddie to invest his faith in him. Freddie accepts the idea that 'The Cause' represents the home he so desperately seeks. He doesn't possess the stability to find real solace in a post-war world; the trauma of his experience renders everything illusory. Thus he accept false-solace from the Master—and from liquor. Anderson invests himself completely in this false-solace by deliberately conjuring another flawed god to reinforce the premise that post-war trauma is plagued by demons.

One last aspect of this 'flawed god' dynamic should be mentioned. Much has been made of the fact that L. Ron Hubbard, the man who created the movement known as the films of p.t. anderson

Scientology, is the likely basis for Lancaster Dodd. That may be true, but it is not relevant to this interpretation. Indeed, one can well assess 'The Master' without having any knowledge whatsoever of L. Ron Hubbard, or Scientology, or any other movement. Anderson's film is much more interested in the uncertainty of post-war experience than in documenting a particular cult. More importantly, the heart of the story here is not Lancaster Dodd, it's Freddie. He completely embodies everything the film aspires to say about the trauma of war.

*

Like 'There Will Be Blood,' 'The Master' opens on an elemental image: the turbulent churning of the ocean. This image is matched by assertive string-music, again provided by the talented Jonny Greenwood. Immediately this combination of harrowing sound and chaotic picture sets the tone of the film. Rough waters lie ahead. The next shot focuses on the film's protagonist, Freddie Quell, peering over the deck of a gunship. His gaze is pensive, uncertain. He only allows his eyes to come up to the rail of the ship, ready to draw back at the first sign of danger. This image suggests a psychology born of fear and trepidation. It's a defensive posture, one which informs Freddie's character throughout the film. He's always uncertain about the world around him, and always prepared to run from it.

The first few minutes of the film cut quickly from one disturbing scene to another. Freddie is shown concocting alcoholic drinks from odd sources — raw fuel, plant extract, etc. He masturbates openly, climbs trees for no reason, and describes the best method for removing crabs from pubic hair. Most disturbing of all is his repeated, aggressive, copulation with a woman made of sand. This sand-figure forms a touchstone of the film; an image returned to time and again by Anderson to portray the illusory nature of love throughout the film. It's a sad and tragic symbol; one which proclaims openly that Freddie will not encounter love in the 'real' sense; rather his sense of solace lies with phantoms. The woman of sand is an icon for the 'elusiveness' of post-war peace; meaning that every source of potential comfort for Freddie is temporary, fleeting, and devoid of substance.

Returning home, Freddie is subjected to psychological tests by the Navy. He is asked to identify abstract blots of ink. To him, everything resembles male and female genitalia; coitus; sexual penetration. Freddie is shown to be emotionally and mentally unbalanced. Another doctor mentions a 'crying spell,' to which Freddie reluctantly admits: "I believe I suffered from. . . nostalgia." His behavior suggests distraction and indifference. He does not follow orders, and can't control his abusive temper. Freddie is arguably the most unlikable of all Anderson's major characters. Only his status as a returning war-veteran evokes the viewer's genuine sympathy. At the same time, this very fact make Freddie a most compelling figure. His trauma conjures the most basic questions about war and its consequences. Why must this man who fought for his country suffer so deeply? This is the premise of Anderson's tragic narrative. His sole intent is to portray one man's wandering through purgatory — not heaven or hell, but the limbo in-between. This is a world of illusion beset by demons, and Freddie is a desolate figure seeking a way to escape his massive suffering.

Eventually Freddie lands a job. The year is 1950. He begins working as a portrait photographer in a well-appointed department store. Yet even here, in a stable environment, Freddie cannot find security. His restlessness begins to manifest itself through agitated behavior. Appropriately enough, the song Anderson uses to usher in this early scene is 'Get Thee Behind Me Satan,' underscoring the sense that Freddie's world is demon-afflicted. He flirts with a floor-model, and sneaks her into a back room to ply her with liquor. The woman is never named; nor does it matter. She is a sexual object to Freddie; incapable of filling the emotional void he harbors. No connection exists because she is unreal. The nature of photography itself emphasizes his illusory situation. Photography is the depiction of a subject, not the subject itself. Here, Freddie has taken a job which idealizes people through representation, denying him true human interaction. In a key scene he literally forces the studio lights into the face of an impatient subject, almost as if the man is not real—holding him up to the light to confirm his actual existence: "You must understand, I want to get the lighting right," he declares. Not surprisingly the man responds by pushing Freddie away, and a brawl ensues. Extreme physical violence comes easily to Freddie; a sudden release of suppressed frustration that matches his feelings of disquiet; of being trapped in a world that grants no peace.

Freddie continues to find retreat in concoctions of alcohol, further numbing himself to reality. In many ways, Freddie renders himself incapable of finding the peace he so desperately seeks. His inability to summon inner-strength is crucial to understanding his later devotion to the Master. So devastated is Freddie, so shell-shocked by war, that he's lost the ability to define for himself a sense of direction. Until he meets Lancaster Dodd, Freddie is an aimless vessel always propelled by a blind desire to run.

Wandering again, he finds work as a field-laborer in California. It is hard work, and at the end of the day Freddie surrounds himself with co-workers willing to share his homemade brew. The spirit is potent, and an old man passes out after drinking it. His fellow workers believe the man is dead, or dying, and accuse Freddie of poisoning him. He denies it, and a fight breaks out. Again, Freddie is forced to run. This haunting shot is one of a handful of defining images in the film: Freddie running breathlessly across a vast expanse of land; directionless, frantic, desperate to escape. Dire questions loom: Escape from what? And to where?

It is here that Freddie meets Lancaster Dodd. The encounter happens by chance. It is night. Along the dock Freddie passes a small ship maneuvering out to open water. Hearing sounds that suggest a celebration, Freddie leaps aboard to join the commotion. Before cutting to the next scene, Anderson fixes on the image of a bridge, suggesting a link between two entities. The next morning, still aboard the ship, Freddie finds himself laying on a bunk. Having passed out the previous night, he now stands confronted by the Master. The two men eye each other curiously. "Why all the skulking and sneaking?" the Master asks. Philip Seymour Hoffman brings to this figure a combination of lively attributes. He is charismatic, well-spoken, and impressively self-assured. At the same time he is chubby, pale, and boyish. By choosing Hoffman to play this odd character, Anderson (who could have chosen, say, Daniel Day Lewis) is carefully depicting Dodd as both commanding and clownish. The result is a pitch-perfect representation of 'flawed god;' part deity, part buffoon.

The two begin conversing, and immediately they sense a connection. We feel it too. There is something oddly compelling about the Master and Freddie. This is not surprising, given that Anderson's films are replete with father-figures and wayward youths brought together by divine intervention. The chance encounter here is not unlike that between, say, Jack Horner and Eddie Adams. Yet here the stakes are much higher, each yearning to make sense of their world in different ways. Further, Lancaster Dodd is Anderson's most complex depiction of a flawed god; literally the head of his own invented religion. Unlike earlier depictions, the dynamic between flawed god and lost man is here presented within a much more devilish atmosphere. This god incarnates a persistent demon—both to Freddie and Anderson. Indeed, Anderson's 'falling back' on this theme itself suggests the trapped ego so consistent with our definition of purgatory. It is a limbo; a world between worlds.

Freddie learns that the ship belongs to Dodd. His daughter, Elizabeth Dodd, is about to be married to a man named Clark. The occasion is joyful and Freddie is invited to stay. Lancaster tells him very clearly: "Come and join us. Leave your worries behind; they'll be there when you get back. And your memories aren't invited." Freddie then meets the Master's son, Val, and his wife, Peggy. She's every bit as aggressive—perhaps more so—than the Master himself. All of them are committed to an organization called 'The Cause,' which expounds Lancaster Dodd's philosophies. Principal among these is the belief that past existences inform our present understanding. Anderson's choice of naming this group 'the Cause' is interesting because 'cause' has more than one meaning. It can refer to a movement, but it can also mean the root source of some ailment. Although he doesn't know it yet, 'the Cause' will indeed become a source of turbulence and uncertainty for Freddie. Notably these early scenes occur on a ship (called 'Alethia,' which ironically means 'truth'), lending to the sense of instability and unsure footing. Compounding this instability is the Master's enthusiasm for Freddie's alcohol. He seems enthralled by it. By making him so vulnerable to their charms, Anderson again shows the Master to be something of a reprobate. He wantonly trades his sensory perception for the blind euphoria of drunkenness.

Before long, Freddie begins to feel comfortable with the Master. He reveals some of his shattered psychology during a question-and-answer session referred to as 'Informal Processing.' The inquiry is aggressive, intrusive, and above all repetitive. Dodd breaks Freddie down, forcing him to reveal hidden aspects of himself. We learn Freddie's father is dead, his mother is institutionalized, he enjoyed sex with his aunt, and killed Japanese soldiers during the war. Most importantly Freddie reveals the existence of someone he deeply loves. This figure, Doris, is the only person for whom he expresses this most basic human emotion. Freddie refers to her as: "the best girl I ever met—the girl I'm going to marry someday." The Master presses harder, demanding to know why they're not together: "Why aren't you with that lovely girl?" Freddie replies helplessly: "I'm a idiot!" The Master drills deeper: "Is she the love of your life? Then why don't you go back to her?" Freddie screams: "I don't know!" This scene shows Joaquin Phoenix as an actor of depth and intensity, contorting his face, his voice, his very being into the broken figure Freddie must be. Yes, Doris exists. But like so many other harbors of solace, she is unreachable; illusory. One is reminded of Kafka's famous phrase: 'Yes there is hope, but not for us.'

The scene dissolves to Freddie's reminiscence of Doris. She is much younger; both lovely and innocent. Anderson presents her as an ideal woman, heightening the sense that she symbolizes a saving grace for Freddie. Seeing her together with him in this sequence is comforting because he appears so much less agitated, even content, in her presence. At this point the potential still exists for Freddie to find some happiness with her. It's the one moment in the entire film where love and solace lay fully within his reach. She even acquiesces to Freddie's desires — agreeing not to go to Norway after he insists she stay. The scene is disarming, showing us a Freddie we don't fully recognize. It's also tragic. Their relationship falls apart under the weight of Freddie's instability, brought about by the burden of war. So disoriented has Freddie become that he's incapable of attaining the very happiness he craves — even in its proximity. In the context of Anderson's films, this scene is especially heartbreaking. Previously he allowed even his most emotionally damaged figures some access to requited love. But not Freddie. He returns to war, kissing Doris goodbye in the middle of the night. He promises to return to her. They will never meet again. The Master ends his harrowing interrogation by telling Freddie: "You're the bravest boy I've ever met." These words possess a well-rehearsed inflection, ostensibly rewarding Freddie's tumultuous purge.

*

The narrative returns to the principal setting, 1950. The Master and his entourage arrive in New York, Freddie among them. Here he witnesses the Master's social milieu: high society figures who routinely assemble lavish gatherings in well-appointed homes. The opulence of these surroundings is strange to Freddie. Attending one of their gatherings, he wanders through the house devoid of certainty. He considers stealing a small female figurine, but can't fit it into his pocket—further symbolizing a frustrated connection to women. The people roaming this place are an illusion cloaked in the garb of material wealth; themselves finders of false-comfort. They partake of The Master's 'Cause' in much the same way they indulge in exotic clothes, or jewelry. To them 'The Cause' is little more than a spiritually chic accessory.

This scene is revelatory, marking the first instance where the Master is openly challenged. An uninvited guest acting as a journalist interrupts Lancaster while he's reviving an elderly woman from a trance. The Master dazzles her with talk of past lives and alternate identities. The reporter, John More, asks Dodd if this ritual isn't simple hypnosis, if 'The Cause' isn't in fact a cult, and whether or not The Master's methods can truly cure Leukemia. The confrontation is pointed and tense. Ill-tempered, the Master quickly descends to profanity: "If you already know the answers to your questions then why ask, pig fuck!!" The outburst is ugly, and the confrontation irks Freddie. He hurls a piece of fruit at the reporter, showing himself a willful defender of the Master.

Later, Freddie confronts Mr. More in his apartment and assaults him.

Freddie becomes immersed in 'The Cause,' giving himself over completely to Dodd's authority. Strangely, even though he's made a home for himself among this bizarre group, he cultivates no sense of kinship among its members. In fact, they seem just as devoid of certainty as he is. One of the most harrowing scenes in any of Anderson's films occurs at just this point. Like so many of his previous films, the middle of the narrative marks the beginning of a descent. In 'The Master' this moment is grotesque and intimate — meant for Freddie's eyes alone.

The scene begins innocently, with Dodd standing amid a gathering of wealthy followers. He begins to sing a crass rendition of 'Go Roving' — the performance filled with caricature and broad gesture. The Master's charisma is particularly pungent here. But amid the merriment, a surreal vision: Freddie is suddenly shown each of these figures in all their imperfection; their naked bodies revealed for him alone to see. This bizarre moment incarnates a human purgatory, a hellish vision packed with stripped souls. The flesh is flaccid; these specimens seem sick. Matching the nausea of the image is the ludicrous song. 'Go Roving' as sung by Hoffman (in what must be the centerpiece of his acting in the film) emerges as a macabre dance filled with bloated vocal contortion. It calls to mind the carnival exorcism performed by Eli Sunday in 'There Will Be Blood.' Only here, there's no one to tell the Master: "That was one goddamn hell of a show." Rather, Freddie seems captivated by this most profane vision, absorbing it like warm liquor.

The next scene presents an even more upsetting image. Upstairs, the Master and Peggy are preparing for bed. He's brushing his teeth over the sink, and she appears behind him. Without warning she grabs his penis and begins stroking it. This act of sexual 'intimacy' between them reveals no love, no symbiosis, no romantic inclination whatsoever. Instead Peggy uses sex as a weapon, scolding Dodd over his affairs with other women and demanding he stay away from Freddie: "No more of that boy's hooch, do you understand!?" He complies even as he ejaculates into her hand. Anderson shrewdly veils the scene, permitting us only to see it from behind (which only heightens its grotesquery in our minds). Again, this is a hellish conception. It reveals the emotional void between Dodd and Peggy, and confirms the sense that 'The Cause' is no haven of spiritual comfort. The viewer is beginning to grasp a truism that eludes Freddie: There's no solace for him here because there's no solace, period.

Things go from bad to worse. The next morning Freddie encounter Val, Dodd's son, on the porch. Val reveals to Freddie that he doesn't place any faith in his father's philosophy, stating flatly: "He's making all this up as he goes along." Freddie reacts badly to the assertion; nearly assaulting Val. Before he can, however, a patrol car arrives at the house. Two policemen approach, asking to see Lancaster Dodd. They have a warrant for his arrest. It seems he embezzled some money from a wealthy donor. Tempers flare as The Master is taken into custody; the exchange becomes heated and physical. Freddie wrestles the officers to the ground in yet another animal outburst; inevitably he too is led away in handcuffs. The scene crackles with emotional tension as now the Master's followers must bear witness to his deceit and corruption. This is no pristine figure, but a man of moral flaw. For Freddie, this revelation hits especially hard.

The sequence Anderson fashions next is arguably the centerpiece of the film. The Master and Freddie are locked in two separate jail-cells, side by side, creating a bifurcated image with each figure occupying half of the visual space. One figure is perfectly still; reflective. The other figure is explosive, physically thrusting himself over and over against the metal bunk, kicking through the porcelain toilet, unleashing a furious tirade against the Master. This image depicts the fundamental dynamic in the film: the flawed god and his disciple, locked together, confronting each other face-to-face. On one level it's a Jekyll-and-Hyde moment, un-masking two vastly different sides of human behavior. On another level, it's Anderson expressing intense frustration with this dynamic; perhaps exhausted by its presence in so much of his art. Like the staged confrontation between Daniel and Eli in 'There Will Be Blood,' this moment again seems a proxy for Anderson facing down his own artistic demon.

Yet here the balance of power is strikingly different. Daniel Plainview routinely dominated Eli Sunday. He physically defeated and eventually murdered him. Here, the opposite is true, with the flawed god in total control of both himself and Freddie. This scene conveys Freddie's absolute helplessness. He can only body forth in useless rage. He can't touch Lancaster Dodd, who stands unmoved in his jail-cell, lecturing: "Your fear of capture and imprisonment is an implant from millions of years ago." This, even as Freddie screams: "Shut the fuck up! You're making this shit up! You make this shit up!" His intense purge exposes the frustration he feels for both the Master and the world itself. The balm for his disquiet, the comfort for his war-torn psychology, is nowhere to be found. It's not in his alcohol; nor is it in the divine figure of Lancaster Dodd. Yet these two—Freddie and the Master—are locked together; trapped in the same purgatory from which neither can escape. The trauma of war has left Freddie so distraught that he's lost all sense of reality. Instead, he wanders an illusory limbo beset by demons. He cannot escape them. He hasn't the emotional capacity or certitude. The strain of divine intervention at work here is very dark, leading Freddie into an ever deepening void.

Throughout the film Anderson composes his images with great care. He sculpts every scene to convey only the most basic emotions experienced by his characters. It is one of the most tightly controlled of all his films, reminiscent of the focus he displayed in 'Punch Drunk Love.' Like that film, 'The Master' revolves around the dynamic between just two characters: Freddie and Lancaster Dodd. Peripheral figures abound, most notably Peggy and Doris. Other characters contribute to our understanding of motive and personality; but ultimately what this cruel scene in the jail-cell reveals is Anderson's precise focus on these two men and their dysfunctional attachment to one another. He follows Freddie's actions so closely that the viewer is nearly repulsed; yet there are few characters in any of Anderson's films who so thoroughly demand the camera's attention. Every inner-flaw, every demented act, every ugly outburst is presented with documentary precision. Anderson hides nothing. His personal investment in Freddie is uncomfortably deep—so deep one must wonder how closely he identifies with war-shattered figures.

The confrontation between Freddie and the Master produces absolutely no resolution. Nor could it. The entire crux of the film rests on the irreconcilable nature of Freddie's plight. The war has left him too damaged to find a home. It's left him devoid of the tools he needs to secure personal peace. For him, there can be no closure, no redemption, no love. Everything in this post-war purgatory is confusing and illusory. Thus, it makes sad sense that in the aftermath of incarceration, Freddie goes back to the Master. He cannot escape his domain. The hellish terms of their existence demand they remain tied to one another. Significantly, none of the other members of 'The Cause' believe in Freddie's commitment. Peggy, Clark, Elizabeth—they all implore the Master to expel him from their midst. Dodd, however, believes Freddie is exactly right for their movement: "For if we are not helping him, it is *we* who have failed."

Freddie is again subjected to a battery of initiation rituals, this time called 'Applications.' These psychological challenges are as pointless as they are grueling. Peggy bombards him with sexual innuendo, checking his reaction. Clark levels insults against him, assessing his temper. Most stressful of all is a test that forces Freddie to walk back and forth between two points—a wall and a window—over and over again, describing each plane while his eyes remain closed. This particular test perfectly depicts the trapped nature of his character. He's caught between two worlds: one represented by the window, teeming with sunlight; the other represented by a wall, a physical obstruction. This is Anderson's metaphor for limbo. Freddie is consigned to the purgatory between Heaven and Hell; unable to pass into one or the other. His world is an uncertain middle-ground. He has yet to encounter anything stable or comforting; finding neither home nor resolution. In this exercise — as in life — he moves blindly between two planes; one sacred and one profane. Guiding his every move is the Master. This image, like the earlier image of Freddie running across a vast expanse of open field, is defining. From it one can extrapolate the entire film. 'The Master' is the portrayal of man trapped in a post-war purgatory. Not Heaven, not Hell, but the illusion in-between. The psychological devastation of war has disrupted his footing. He's completely unbalanced. At one point he deliriously proclaims: "I can leave anytime I want, but I choose to stay here!!" In this moment, his loss of control — his gathering frustration — is palpable. The sense that Freddie will run from this dark place is overwhelming.

The scene shifts to Phoenix; a city whose name portends resurrection. Outside the urban sprawl, amid the sweltering desert, the Master takes Freddie to a secret location. There they unearth the Master's life work: an unpublished manuscript that embodies the very philosophy of 'The Cause.' Like buried treasure the document is mined from the earth — even as Dodd surveys the terrain for would-be thieves. The paranoia here is unwarranted, but convincing. Dodd's book, 'The Split Saber,' is meant to be a revolutionary tract; one intended to place him alongside the great thinkers of the world. Oddly, Freddie seems both attentive and aloof. He exhibits a workmanlike relationship to the Master, but evinces less emotional commitment than before. He helps manicure the Master's image; photographing him in just the right light, with just the right expression of thoughtfulness. 'The Cause' must be carefully packaged for a new generation of consumers.

The Master speaks to a small gathering of followers. Afterward a benefactor named Helen approaches him. She wants to know why the wording of his doctrine has changed from 'recall' to 'imagine.' Previously 'The Cause' asked its followers to 'recall' their past existences; now they are merely asked to 'imagine' past existences. She points out the vastly different implications of each: one asks its followers to remember what is real, the other asks only to pretend that it might be. The Master erupts at the confrontation: "What do you want, Helen!!" Meanwhile, another follower tells Freddie that 'The Split Saber' is no good; the whole thing should be chopped down to a three-page pamphlet. Freddie leads the man outside and assaults him physically. In both of these instances the seams of 'The Cause' are beginning to come apart. Whatever the original intent, the movement has devolved into a cult. The false nature of this movement mirrors the false-world Freddie roams; both devoid of real meaning.

The yearning to run, to escape, begins to manifest in Freddie. As a returning veteran, shell-shocked on so many levels, he's spent the duration of the film escaping from one false-world into another. In no instance (save the moments together with Doris) does he encounter love or solace. Freddie has invested himself completely in the Master, yet he still feels bereft of spiritual calm. Even at this late point in the narrative he channels frustration through violence, and remains emotionally removed from every other character. In the jail-cell scene earlier, Dodd tells Freddie: "I'm the only one who likes you! The only one!" Indeed, a fair question arises: Why is Freddie still unable to make any meaningful human connection?

*

The film enters the third act. By this point in every one of Anderson's films some semblance of resolution begins to coalesce around the main characters: John and Clementine have returned home to Sydney; Dirk has received absolution from Jack Horner; Officer Jim and Claudia have enjoyed their first kiss; Barry Egan has settled his score with the Mattress Man; and H.W. Plainview has married Mary Sunday. But here, Freddie Quell is every bit as confused, alone, and emotionally unfulfilled as he was at the film's beginning. Why? Because 'The Master' is an absolute tragedy; one that considers the effects of war in relation to total human loss. The very seriousness of the subject demands a commitment to tragic depiction. It's not that Freddie hasn't found inner-peace; it's that he *can't* find inner-peace. That's why, even at this late point in the film, he continues to wander without making any meaningful connection. The war has left him so damaged that he — alone of all Anderson's main characters — will find no resolution, no love, and no human solace whatsoever.

No wonder then that Freddie needs only the slightest incentive to run yet again. The scene shifts once more to a vast expanse of open land. Earlier in the film, that expanse was an endless field of lettuce; here it's the broad Arizona desert. The

Master, Peggy, and Freddie engage in a casual mental exercise. They are each asked to choose a point in the distance, and impose upon that point an imagined goal. Then each of them are tasked to reach this point on a motorcycle, and return. It's a simple game meant to signify the attainment of whatever goal the rider envisions. Again this brings up a serious question: What is Freddie's 'point?' More philosophically, what is the point to his unfulfilled existence? The answer, on one level, is that there's no point to Freddie. Thus, there is no conceivable point in the distance which might represent a goal for him. To envision a goal, one must have a sense of direction. Freddie has none. So when his turn comes, he simply mounts the motorcycle and rides. At terrific velocity, Freddie roars into the horizon until he completely disappears. He doesn't return because he hasn't discovered his 'point.' This self-reflective exercise grants Freddie the opportunity to escape yet again. He will not be rediscovered until the Master tracks him down much later.

At the same time, on a more tangible level, there is (and has always been) one point for Freddie: Doris. The next scene takes him back to her house after so many years absence. She's the only solace he has ever known; his one true love. In pursuing his 'point,' Freddie wholeheartedly envisions Doris — the ideal woman — as its embodiment. Sadly, Doris too has become an illusion. Freddie is informed by her mother that she's now married and living in Alabama. Freddie is wounded by the news. He displays confusion; he can't wrap his mind around this unjust circumstance. That she wasn't still waiting for him all these years later perplexes him, further underscoring the degree to which he is truly misguided. She will never become Mrs. Doris Quell; rather her name now is Doris Day. This too suggests her idealized position in the film; so openly matched to an icon of feminine purity. Like so many other milestones of Freddie's journey, Doris has become unreachable. The Master asked him to imagine a point in the distance, and like every other point Freddie has sought, this one too is a figment. The outcome here is tragically appropriate: Freddie cannot attain anything real because he lacks human substance himself. He knows no certainty of any kind, robbed of it by the devastation of war.

Freddie wanders away from this heartbreaking revelation completely defeated. He takes refuge in a darkened theater where a final instance of divine intervention awaits him. Not since 'Magnolia' has Anderson conceived so abstract, so inexplicable, so impossible an instance of divine representation as occurs in this scene. In 'Magnolia,' the fantastic rain of frogs symbolized an imposition of godly will. It was a monumental gesture meant to provide human connection and resolution to a multitude of characters. In 'The Master,' the device Anderson constructs is every bit as abstract and mysterious. The crucial distinction here is that the device fosters no comfort, no resolution, and no hope whatsoever. In fact, this unexpected call only succeeds in drawing Freddie deeper into the void.

Appropriately, the theater is pitch black. On the screen plays a Casper cartoon. Casper the Friendly Ghost; a phantom of helpful inclination. From nowhere, an usher brings Freddie a telephone. Bewildered, he takes the phone and listens. It's the Master's voice he hears; a haunting intonation from a distant land. England in fact, halfway across the world. Consider the impossibility of the situation. The year is 1950, and from England Lancaster Dodd has decided to call Freddie. He has no idea where he is; nor could he possibly conceive that Freddie might be in a movie theater. Further, the Master would have to know the phone number to this obscure theater, and convince the usher to find Freddie. And how could the usher possibly know who Freddie is? Yet he never speaks Freddie's name — he simply hands him the phone. All of this (not to mention the seven hour time-difference between America and England) contributes to an absolutely impossible scenario.

Yet it makes perfect sense. Freddie inhabits a purgatory existence surrounded by ghostly figures. Now his demon has found him. This moment of divine intervention is literal — it even occurs in the presence of a cinematic phantom: Casper the Friendly Ghost. He and his playmate seek buried treasure, not unlike the scene earlier when the Master and Freddie unearthed his manuscript. Casper exclaims on-screen: "The Captain never leaves the ship!" And indeed, Freddie's captain hasn't left either. He reaches out to Freddie from the ether itself, calling him to England, commanding him back to his side. The words he uses are the most blunt Anderson has ever chosen to articulate the dynamic between flawed god and lost man. The Master begins: "I miss you." Freddie responds in a tone that suggests both terror and longing: "How did you find me?" To which the Master replies: "We're tied together." This bald declaration is the sum of all Anderson's divinely inspired god/man relationships. The lost man is always tied to the flawed god in a manner that seems inescapable. In his previous films, that relationship generally led to some positive resolution for one or the other. Here, the distinction could not be more profound: Freddie is being drawn back to the Master as a continued form of persecution. No closure, no peace, no absolution will come of their reunion. It is near the end of the film, and still Freddie has encountered nothing real, or meaningful, in this purgatory existence. His post-war trauma has defeated every quest for peace; every yearning for home.

This last point is considerable. In all of Anderson's prior films the concept of 'home' is strong. The notion of homecoming is a touchstone of his art; one he routinely conjures as a harbor for intangible themes of redemption, forgiveness, and love. John and Clementine return home to Reno at the end of 'Hard Eight.' Dirk returns to the home of Jack Horner at the end of 'Boogie Nights.' Frank Mackie returns to his father's home at the end of 'Magnolia.' Barry Egan returns to Lena's home at the end of 'Punch Drunk Love.' And Eli Sunday returns to the home of Daniel Plainview to meet his ultimate end in 'There Will Be Blood.' But in 'The Master,' so powerful is the theme of disconnect that Freddie only wanders further from home. He stumbles through his personal purgatory as though following an outward spiral. From the war in the Pacific, to mainland America, to faraway England, his sense of 'home' is constantly disrupted.

The very next image is the same turbulent ocean that opened the film. Freddie arrives in England, unable to deny his Master, and meets Lancaster Dodd once again. They speak politely, then Freddie mentions his 'dream.' This dream is actually the previous scene in the movie theater, which Freddie confuses with something illusory — appropriately so, given his inability to distinguish reality from unreality. His post-war purgatory is very much a bad dream; a vile illusion. The Master looks Freddie in the eye and renders his final sentence — a punctuation mark to his prior intimations in the movie theater: "Go to that landless latitude and good luck; for if you figure a way to live without serving a master—any master—then let the rest of us know, will you? For you'd be the first person in the history of the world." Here Anderson allows his flawed god to inflict a lasting judgment on Freddie; an anti-declaration of independence. The Master is telling him that escape is impossible—he will always loom over Freddie's roaming figure. It's a terrifying pronouncement, one that pushes this lopsided dynamic almost to the point of mockery. Far from summoning words of comfort, the Master strikes a tone that implies damnation. Freddie has found no redemption in this final encounter. No forgiveness, no love, and no peace.

In the last two scenes of the film, Freddie's inability to find love—that paragon of human redemption—is depicted in the most heartbreaking manner. In the penultimate scene Freddie meets an English girl in a local pub. The two inevitably retire to her flat. Instead of allowing any display of romantic promise between them, Anderson depicts them in bed together, indulging in crude sex, while Freddie performs the same 'Informal Processing' on her that the Master practiced on him: "Say your name. Say it again. No blinking. If you blink, you fail. Infringement!" It's a pitiful display, one that only confirms how deeply disfigured Freddie has become. He's little more than a pale imitation of the Master. A shadow. He tells the young woman: "You're the bravest girl I've ever met."

The very last image of the film is more brutal still. It depicts Freddie laying beside a woman of sand, embracing that which so utterly defines the emptiness of his war-torn existence. For Freddie the only solace is illusion; the only love is a proxy. He's become a figment; one whose most intimate companions are figments too. It's especially heartbreaking that Freddie's final refuge is found in a woman of sand because it symbolizes the absence of human love. In this lonely scene he's completely deprived of any true connection; any lasting peace. The two figures seem little more than detritus waiting to be claimed by a careless sea.

The film ends without any closure for Freddie. We know not whether he escapes the Master, or discovers love. The implication is that neither will occur. By far, this is Anderson's most desolate portrayal of human resolution. In every one of his previous films he made room for redemption through requited love or personal accomplishment. Not here. Freddie is accorded nothing. Every action yields disillusion from the beginning of the film to the end. His is a hellish drama, darkly depicting the purgatory endured by war-ravaged veterans.

Like John Ford's 'Let There Be Light,' the film itself is an homage to the war-veteran — those who do so much for so little. As suggested before, one can draw a parallel to Martin Scorsese's Travis Bickle, the veteran of Vietnam consigned to his own purgatory. Yet Freddie Quell is more forsaken still, and 'The Master' much more tragic. At least Travis Bickle found some redemption through Iris. Freddie secures no personal redemption whatsoever. His war-torn past leaves him crippled both emotionally and psychologically. The demons that pervade his post-war purgatory prey on him relentlessly, consigning him to an unending state of personal frustration. Freddie's struggle lends ultimate depth to Jimmy Gator's durable phrase: "The Book says we might be through with the past, but the past ain't through with us."

Anderson's mature tragedy is made all the more hellish by its inescapability. Freddie is destined to be a figure forever trapped between two planes, one composed of clear light, one of solid wall. One can imagine him (and perhaps Anderson too) still moving back and forth between those two defining planes, blindly struggling to describe what he feels, impelled by an unseen Master.

Part Seven:

SO NOW, WHAT THEN

*

P. T. Anderson's filmmaking is best understood in relation to biblical symbolism. When filtered through instances of fate or chance, this symbolism takes the distinct shape of divine intervention. Anderson has consistently fashioned his cinema around this persistent theme, populating his films with what I call 'flawed gods and lost men.' Divine intervention is the motivating force which brings his characters together and determines their ultimate reward (or punishment). In the majority of his films this reward generally consists of personal redemption through forgiveness or requited love. Anderson's concept of divinity is carefully shaped to fit his own ironic sensibility. Most often the gods of his narratives are ill-equipped to offer meaningful guidance. By extension, Anderson's films suggest a certain suspicion of the godhead. This fascination with divine intervention and biblical symbolism does not define Anderson's cinema as overtly religious, rather it implies an aesthetic comprehension of ageless themes. These lend durability to his theater. As a storyteller, Anderson prefers broad dramatic gestures—big images—conveyed through everyday figures whose struggles nearly always proceed from discovery, to loss, to personal resolution. The manifestation of divine intervention in his films has evolved over time to become more confrontational, and more personal. The tragic nature of his most recent film in particular suggests a profound emotional investment in the subject-matter. His six major films also show a progressive sophistication; becoming more ideologically complex with each successive work. Finally, a deepening physical intensity has also marked the growth of his cinema.

In assessing Anderson's body of work, it's useful to begin with a broad overview. His first two shorts, 'The Dirk Diggler Story,' and 'Cigarettes and Coffee,' belong to an experimental period. Neither film exemplifies the subtle tone of optimism that mark his major films; nor do they exhibit a willingness to grant any character solace or requited love. As a motivating force, divine intervention is almost nonexistent; although the biblical symbolism in 'Cigarettes and Coffee' portends much for Anderson's later films. Of course, these two shorts were not designed to be full-length narratives, thus their miniature length exempts them from the same level of scrutiny given to his major films. They are the work of a young artist, and should be seen as preliminary sketches for later, larger, cinematic portraits.

In fact Anderson's first two major films are born out of those early shorts. 'Hard Eight' and 'Boogie Nights' appeared within a short span of only two years; as such they share much in common. Both reveal a strong commitment to divine intervention as a motivating force. For John, Sydney is delivered unexpectedly; just as Jack Horner meets Eddie Adams through no premeditated action. Both films involve the unmistakable presence of flawed gods and lost men. Sydney is flawed by way of his past sins; Jack through his affiliation with a socially deviant enterprise. John and Eddie are lost in the sense that neither man knows how to secure personal fulfillment. Yet in both films the sense of resolution is strong. Here Anderson grants his characters forgiveness, redemption, and requited love. Both films also bequeath a quiet optimism in the wake of suffering. In keeping with the argument for artistic progression, it should be noted that 'Boogie Nights' displays a filmmaking technique that outclasses 'Hard Eight' on almost every level.

Similarly, 'Magnolia' outclasses 'Boogie Nights.' Not only is the level of artistry more sophisticated, but characters are drawn with greater depth. The enormity of 'Magnolia,' and the skill displayed in moving so many figures from dark to light, makes a massive impression. For many, it is Anderson's highest accomplishment as a filmmaker. It combines aspects of his previous work to form a summation of everything the artist had learned to that point in time. The great rain of frogs itself (perhaps the ultimate biblical symbol in any of his films) reveals an artist whose representation of divinity had assumed a masterful abstraction. There is nothing in his previous films to match the scale of utterance in 'Magnolia,' nor does any of his prior work display so deep a personal investment in the name of artistic growth.

There are two films that truly stand apart when assessing Anderson's major canon. The first is 'Punch Drunk Love.' Here the director returns to a more intimate scale, paring the film down to two major characters, Barry and Lena; and bridging them with a third, the mysterious harmonium. What makes the film distinct is the absence of flawed gods. Unlike John in 'Hard Eight' or Dirk in 'Boogie Nights,' or Frank Mackie in 'Magnolia,' Barry Egan suffers the guidance of no towering person. Over the course of the film he becomes the architect of his own fortune. Only at the beginning of the film, when the harmonium is deposited in the street without explanation, does the specter of divine intervention appear. But in truth, Barry determines his own actions for the sake of Lena Leonard. 'Punch Drunk Love' is Anderson's testament to the discovery of free will, and an homage to the redemptive power of requited love. In no other film are those two defining principles so purposefully entwined, or so unapologetically championed. The artistic growth evinced in this small film is not the velocity of its images, but the conviction of its ideas.

Barry Egan's breakthrough to free will informs the next major character in Anderson's cinema. Daniel Plainview is indeed a paragon of decisiveness — more imperially self-assured than any prior protagonist. Unique to this film, Anderson conceives the main character for one artistic purpose: to obliterate the very concept of divine intervention by murdering its symbolic agent, Eli Sunday. 'There Will Be Blood' represents Anderson's most confrontational depiction of the flawed god/lost man dynamic to this point in time. Indeed, the film is wholly composed around a monumental struggle between sacred and profane figures. Here, the religious allusions are not abstract but literal incarnations. Eli is a preacher; his intervention in Daniel's business is divinely inspired. This marks Anderson's first use of an openly religious figure as the principal antagonist. It also marks the first adaptation of another work in the construction of his script; and the first period-piece in his repertory.

The increased sophistication here comes by way of Anderson's willingness to push his ideas as far as they can go.

Daniel is the ultimate symbol of free will; Eli is the ultimate symbol of divine presence. Their confrontation results in the ultimate act of resolution, namely murder. Further, Anderson's total investment in Daniel Plainview — charging him with the task of destroying an adversarial idea — forms the ultimate artistic gesture. No character in any of Anderson's films can match Daniel's colossal will, and none can match Eli's religious commitment. Nor does any previous film suggest so personal an involvement on the part of the director to defeat his own artistic demons.

The other film which stands apart in Anderson's canon is 'The Master.' This is his most complicated film to date, and the one which most emphatically dispenses with signature themes of emotional closure. Freddie Quell is unlike any of Anderson's characters because he carries with him the trauma of war. Ultimately, 'The Master' is a testament to the war-veteran's emotional and psychological devastation. In fact, the film's sensibility is so disoriented that Anderson purposely revives an old demon, divine intervention, to propel the film's drama. Here the flawed god is conceived on the grandest scale. Lancaster Dodd is perhaps *the* flawed god in all of Anderson's cinema — so flawed that his religion is a cult built entirely around himself. He lies, steals, and drinks wantonly. In no other film is the relationship between flawed god and lost man so egregiously characterized. Anderson is not interested in cloaking his thematic material in subtlety. Here the flawed god is literal, the divine intervention is relentless, and the misdirection is irreversible. The great distinction of 'The Master' is its refusal to grant any emotional resolution to Freddie. He is never allowed the redemption, forgiveness, or homecoming so routinely provided for Anderson's other protagonists. Most tragically of all he is denied any semblance of requited love; left to lie on the beach with a figment of sand.

In this film Anderson deepens his artistry, willfully depicting tragedy in the classic sense; leaving no solace for his distressed creation. In many ways it's Anderson's most mature film, for in no previous work does he allow any character to fall so far. Like 'There Will Be Blood' before it, 'The Master' projects an extremely personal vision, one in which the struggle of the artist is discerned in the difficulty of the finished film. The sense of sacrifice and trauma is strong, revealing a filmmaker increasingly concerned with plumbing the deepest human depths to fashion his art, no matter the personal cost. Little wonder that the length of time required to complete 'The Master' was a full five years—longer than the span of time required to produce his first three films combined.

Another example of the artistic progression in Anderson's films centers on the move toward greater freedom of will. In 'Hard Eight' Anderson painted a portrait of three characters whose every action was a response to some external force; whether that was Sydney's reaction to Jimmy's threat, or John's move to Las Vegas, or Clementine's introduction to John. In 'Boogie Nights,' Anderson fashions a world where the protagonist is almost devoid of will entirely. Eddie Adams meets Jack by chance, and the remainder of his motives are dependent on other characters' actions. Even at the end, his extraordinary dialogue is a reaction to his own reflection. In 'Magnolia,' Anderson begins to respect his characters' freedom of will, allowing some of them a self-determination in the third act of the film. Donnie Smith's decision to rob his bosses, Frank Mackie's decision to see his father, and both Linda and Jimmy's decision to take their own lives—all are motivated by free will. Anderson gives this freedom even greater reign in 'Punch Drunk Love,' granting Barry the decisiveness to pursue Lena in Hawaii (and rewarding him generously for it). In 'There Will Be Blood,' Anderson fashions a figure *defined* by free will. Daniel Plainview moves through the world with no strings attached; nothing guides him but his own titanic ambition. This at the behest of Anderson himself, securing independence for his art.

The only real flaw in this progress-assessment comes in the figure of Freddie Quell. He exhibits no freedom of will whatsoever, guided rather by the direct influence of a defective Master. Here Anderson makes a pronouncement on the absolute trauma of war, burying free will under the damage of shell-shock. Freddie is so disabled, so lost, that he hasn't the inner-fortitude to summon free will. 'The Master' ultimately depicts the human cost of war; refusing the veteran any freedom to find redemption, love, or peace.

*

Many feel the overwhelming theme in Anderson's art is the motif of parental discord. Unquestionably this theme is present; but as an interpretive device it suffers a serious shortcoming in that it fails to show any aesthetic progress within his canon. Consider the family disconnect between John and his father in 'Hard Eight.' This dynamic is unknown. Anderson does not fill in that negative space, making its contextual assessment near-impossible. In his next film, the sense of parental strife is much more clearly drawn, centering principally on Dirk's difficult relationship with his mother. In 'Magnolia,' this theme manifests itself in several characters' lives, most dramatically in the painful kinship between Frank Mackie and Earl Partridge. Now, at this point it might be fair to argue that indeed there *is* a progression of theme within these first three films. The familial dysfunction that barely exists in 'Hard Eight' becomes more pronounced in 'Boogie Nights,' and extremely pronounced in 'Magnolia.' However, that progression hits a brick wall when his next three films are assessed.

In 'Punch Drunk Love,' there's no parental turbulence at all—neither Barry nor Lena's parents are so much as mentioned in the body of the film. And although it might be argued that Barry's sisters represent the theme of defective families, the level of discord between them and Barry is mild when compared to 'Magnolia' or 'Boogie Nights.' As for the artistry itself, the depiction of familial discord here certainly doesn't surpass that presented in Anderson's previous films. This is perhaps the most important point, because an argument centered on parental discord as the thrust of Anderson's development collapses when assessing its evolution within his cinema. By the time one gets to 'There Will Be Blood,' this argument becomes even more convoluted because here the paternal decay revolves around an adoptive relationship. H.W. is not the biological son of Daniel Plainview, nor is he understood in that way by the father. Henry is a false relation as well; a lie manufactured for the sake of personal gain. The familial dysfunction in this film is simply a different version of prior instances of discord, not a more artistically perfect one. In 'The Master' (like 'Punch Drunk Love'), the protagonist's relationship with his parents is not depicted. Freddie's mother and father (along with his aunt) are barely mentioned, and no siblings are ever discussed. He's alone in the world, bereft of any family, which is appropriate to his tragedy. Even to the extent that one might argue the prominent theme of parental substitution throughout Anderson's films (where surrogate parents replace biological ones), it still becomes difficult to successfully argue a progression of artistry within that interpretation.

No, it's Anderson's peculiar relationship to the divine that best reveals his growth as an artist. From the Adam and Eve motif of 'Hard Eight,' through the earthly paradise and fall from grace of 'Boogie Nights,' to the fateful encounters and spiritual rain of 'Magnolia,' to the anti-religious experiment of 'Punch Drunk Love,' to the destruction of divinity in 'There Will Be Blood,' to the omnipotence of 'The Master,' the theme of flawed gods and lost men amid divine intervention has defined his trajectory as a filmmaker.

Anderson's films have grown more deeply personal as well, requiring greater lengths of time to conceive more powerful visions. Throughout his career he's consistently portrayed the truth of human struggle through arduous journeys for redemption. In some instances the reward is triumphant (i.e. Barry and Lena). In other instances it's tragic (i.e. Freddie Quell). Above all, Anderson's preference for building cinema around substantive themes, and his intuitive devotion to biblical symbolism, lend his films an enduring quality.

In the broadest sense it's possible to consider film itself—the medium—as a flawed god which has lured Anderson on a winding odyssey. Because the nature of art is elusive, promising nothing more than the journey itself, the relationship between any artist and his medium is not unlike pursuing a divine influence. The experience contains moments of triumph and despair—not unlike the emotional palette from which Anderson draws his characters. Nothing is guaranteed, and the value of the journey is discerned only in its meaning to the artist. Anderson can do nothing more than follow his own flawed god to whatever work of art the process conceives. The acceptance of fate and chance runs strong among artists, because the serendipity involved in constructing any work of art defies explanation. The faith Anderson invests in his own talent, given to the service of his medium, is not so very different from the faith his characters place in masterful figures. The odyssey itself, to whatever destination, is drama.

His art is unique; there are few filmmakers so well-attuned to the high and low of human experience. When he fashions a tragedy of unrequited love, the emotions resonate with great pathos. When he portrays personal fulfillment, the euphoria is infectious. In darkness and light, in storm and stress, in life and death, P.T. Anderson has conceived images that illuminate our shared pursuit of humanity. He is everyman's Everyman; a champion of that small glimmer of hope buried at the bottom of Pandora's box *and* an auteur of the inescapable hardship that binds us together as mortal figures.

In presenting these arguments, my aim is not to pronounce the last word on Anderson's work. Rather my interpretation is meant to be one voice among a building chorus. To my mind, Anderson deserves the broadest and deepest critique possible given the depth and breadth of his artistry. His cinema is compelling; it casts a spell upon the viewer not unlike that serpent at the door described in the preface. It keeps us rooted; keeps us challenged. His art is visually harrowing and personally generous; it is both epic and intimate. It draws us deep inside, calls our attention to hopeful moments, and in the end leaves us to ponder sudden light.

NOTES

*

Because 'Serpent at the Door' is a work of interpretive criticism, source material for the book comes almost entirely from viewing the films themselves. In some instances external commentary (usually in the form of available interviews with Anderson concerning his various projects) furnished useful insight into the director's motive. A good example of this concerns 'The Master.' For my interpretation, it became important to understand the influence of John Ford's documentary, 'Let There Be Light.' Viewing that film, in turn, provided a solid foundation for approaching a highly complex work. 'The Master' is challenging, and will no doubt continue to generate a myriad of distinct criticism. This particular instance of importing an external influence into my final interpretation, however, proved the exception. In nearly every other instance, I relied on my own instincts to discern common themes and symbols within Anderson's body of work.

The process of assessing Anderson's movies will unquestionably vary from person to person. Given the ready availability of DVD versions of each film (save his two early shorts), the manner by which a given individual immerses himself in Anderson's canon will further affect their interpretation. Viewing the films chronologically, for example, provides a different experience than watching them in random order. Different connections will be made, and a sense of Anderson's cumulative artistry (which in turn speaks to his progressive development) may prove more difficult to pin down when his films are viewed out of succession. A recent video essay by Darren Foley illustrates this point. In it, he assesses 'Punch Drunk Love,' 'There Will Be Blood,' and 'The Master' as P.T. Anderson's "Trilogy." But to properly understand them as such, he insists the films be viewed in the following sequence: 'There Will Be Blood,' then 'The Master,' then 'Punch Drunk Love.' Now, whatever one thinks about the substance of the argument itself, his attempt to link multiple films into a cohesive unit is admirable. There is too little criticism of Anderson's movies that seeks this kind of comprehensive overview. It is further intriguing that he opts to remove the filmmaking process from his interpretation, refusing to acknowledge the order of the films as they were made, instead creating his own continuity to support his argument. Conversely, I chose to interpret Anderson's work chronologically because to me the films show a progressive maturity of expression. The manner by which Anderson understands certain themes—evolving all the while as an artist—progressively shapes his cinema. Thus the pattern in his filmmaking (which is intrinsic to my interpretation) is best discerned when his films are studied sequentially.

In formulating my own argument, I tried as much as possible to insulate myself from other critics' assessments. Not so much because I demand untainted criticism above all else, but rather because studies dedicated to an overview of Anderson's canon are (at this point) quite rare. As of this writing, there are no books in print that attempt a cohesive interpretation of his entire body of work from the short-films through 'The Master.' As such, his art truly needs a diverse body of interpretation to promote an active dialog from which a general consensus may begin to be reached. Independent criticism that eschews external influence is much more likely to produce a unique interpretation, which in turn should contribute to a more diverse conversation. Inevitably there will be some degree of overlap in any two viewers' evaluations—but that overlap should come from similar observations rather than borrowed ones. As stated in my introduction, this book was written with one purpose in mind: to supplement the growing dialog concerning Anderson's remarkable work.

Unfortunately the director himself has provided little assistance to those who wish to develop a cohesive interpretation of his cinema. Although he recorded audio commentary for the DVD versions of both 'Hard Eight,' and 'Boogie Nights,' he rarely mentions thematic structure or symbolism in either. Rather, he generally discusses the actors involved (whom he clearly admires), or technical aspects of the filmmaking process. This is also true for the small documentary entitled 'Magnolia Diary,' which appears on the bonus disc of the DVD release. It is here that Anderson mentions the ominous snake that compelled him to complete the film's screenplay. Similar anecdotes abound throughout the documentary, but very little is mentioned that might inspire a thematic understanding of the film itself. Anderson supplied no further commentaries for any of his subsequent DVD's, and the bonus materials that appear on 'Punch Drunk Love,' 'There Will Be Blood,' and 'The Master'—while interesting—do not offer assessments of theme, metaphor, symbol, or meaning.

This is generally the case with Anderson's many interviews as well. He is not a shy artist. The diligent researcher will encounter dozens of interviews with the director, very few of which touch on the symbolism within his films, or the artistic motives that inform his vision. He is an elusive speaker who tends to dismiss any serious deliberation of metaphor or philosophy (at least within his own films). For those interested in such things, his reluctance to reflect on these aspects of his art can be frustrating. But at the same time it's probably wise, because such remarks often diminish the mystery in a given work. His reticence forces the viewer to do his own thinking, which in the end foments a greater degree of appreciation.

Last but not least, I would strongly encourage any fan of Anderson's—casual or committed—to become familiar with Cigarettes & Red Vines (cigsandredvines.blogspot.com). This website, maintained by CJ Wallis and Cory Everett, is a treasure trove of valuable information concerning Paul Thomas Anderson and his films. It contains a multitude of links to interviews, critical assessment of individual movies, and archived data organized by topic or year (as far back as 1993). Almost every bit of relevant news concerning Anderson and his films (past, present, or future) eventually lands on Cigarettes & Red Vines. As a resource, I've found it both well-organized and comprehensive; an indispensible tool for the writer and reader alike.

S.M., 2013

www.ingramcontent.com/pod-product-compliance
Lightning Source LLC
Chambersburg PA
CBHW030006190526
45157CB00014B/457